LEADING CHANGE AT WORK

THE SECRET STRUCTURE OF CHANGE AND HOW EVERYONE CAN MAKE IT HAPPEN

ADAM BRAUS

Peripatetic Press

555 Post Street

San Francisco, CA 94102

First Printing: 2019

ISBN 9781092964289

Special discounts are available on quantity purchases by corporations, associations, educators, and others. Bookstores, libraries, and wholesalers: please contact Adam Braus at adam.braus@icloud.com.

Dedicated to Kate Schneider-Braus

This world, where much is to be done, and little known...

DR. SAMUEL JOHNSON

CONTENTS

INTRODUCTION: THE PROBLEM WITH TYPE II PROBLEMS

A few years ago, my neighbor Mark was an engineer at Apple, and he was ripe for a promotion. Mark's manager permitted him to take a much-coveted class available only through Apple's internal training program, Apple U. They call the workshop, "What makes Apple, Apple?" It is only open to people who are trending towards upper management.

In the course, the instructors explained Apple's culture. They tried to convey some of the company's accumulated wisdom to an up-and-coming cohort of executives. When the topic turned to leading change, the instructor broke down the challenges that staff and engineers might face into three types: Type I, Type II, and Type III.

A Type I problem is one inside your department over which you have direct control. For example, if you are on the team in charge of many of the creative assets for an upcoming ad campaign for Apple Music, you can decide what those assets look like or how they are shaped and presented. A Type I problem is one most capable workers can solve. It's safe to say you won't be hired at Apple or last more than a few weeks if you can't solve them.

A Type II problem is one over which you have no direct control.

For example, imagine that you are a marketer for Apple Music, and you want your analytics dashboards to show you different metrics. Or imagine you are an engineer on the App Store, and you want to change the policy by which apps get on the store. You might be able to solve these challenges, but you cannot solve them directly because they require communicating and negotiating with others.

A Type III problem is fundamentally impossible. For example, if you try to stop Apple from making iPhones. Practically speaking, no matter what you do, you won't succeed in solving Type III challenges.

"Type II problems make or break people's careers," the Apple instructors said. "If you can't solve Type II problems, you won't make it beyond 18—24 months."

All the challenges you encounter at any organization fit into one of these three types. Mark was already finding his Type I problems pretty challenging, so he wondered how he could get better at solving Type II problems. He buckled into his seat and waited for the trainers to tell him.

But they never did.

The Apple U instructors didn't have much to say. They taught that there was a "special way" to solve Type II problems: some people had it; others didn't. They didn't explain any further. But, being able to solve Type II problems, they assured everyone, would make or break their careers at Apple.

Countless classic business books attempt to teach their readers how to overcome Type II problems, and they are all worth reading. However, they all fall short of a full solution. Many of them ignore the real dynamics of companies and organizations, and few provide a proven step-by-step guide to leading change.

I've interviewed and worked with hundreds of people at all levels of organizations—from facilities to the C-Suite—and everyone is struggling with change. Whether it is making a much-needed update to an outdated workflow, or revolutionizing the whole organization, change is hard.

And the problem is equally as bad for those at the top of organizations as for those at the bottom. If you pick up any copy of *Harvard Business Review*, you'll see how much executives and CEOs struggle with leading change, grappling with Type II problems, and racking their brains for how to make their companies more agile and innovative.

If things weren't hard enough already, organizations and teams are not built to change. Even at organizations full of collaborative people and good managers, innovators can still encounter so many gatekeepers and rules that even common-sense change is daunting. Most organizations are designed to accomplish one task; they are not built to change and adapt.

How can you be expected to make a change in the face of such opposition? Where do you start? What do you do first? Do you go to your manager? Do you corner a VP in an elevator or bend the ear of a colleague over beers? How do you experiment with new ideas while not risking your career and reputation?

People trying to lead change often wander down a series of dead ends. They play politics, flatter people, or throw them under the proverbial bus. Or they go to their managers week after week with their ideas, and yet never make an inch of progress. Change can start to feel impossible and hopeless. If that happens, potential leaders of change become frustrated and apathetic. They switch off the innovative part of their brains at work and apply it elsewhere: in short, they disengage.

A new model for leading change

If you picked up this book, you want to learn how to make a change where you work. You want to fix something that is broken or build something new. It could be something as big as launching a new product, or as small as moving the coffeemaker. You have a brilliant idea or a persistent hunch, and you want to make it real. But leading change is hard. You might feel discouraged or have already given up.

You are not alone, and you have good reason to be frustrated. No one has figured out exactly how to change organizations. While understanding and embracing change is more critical than ever, how to make change consistently remains as elusive as ever.

Most organizations do change in the traditional way: the executive team makes a three-to-five-year plan during an offsite. Maybe they decide to change sales targets, start or end various products, or reorganize the company's departments and people. Change comes down from above and is met with a mixture of surprise, agreement, resistance, and apathy.

Business leaders try their best to make top-down change work, and they are open to suggestions. In 1996 John Kotter published *Leading Change* outlining an eight-step process for making changes to an organization. Kotter's process focuses exclusively on leading change from the top down. Leading change from the top down misses the countless opportunities for innovation, improvement, and—perhaps most importantly—psychological safety and positive culture building, when everyone can make change.

On the other side of Kotter, there is Steve Blank, the author of *The Four Steps to the Epiphany* and his protégé Eric Ries, author of *The Lean Startup*. Blank invented, and Ries promoted, a new sort of organizational change called **Lean Innovation**. Lean innovation focuses on interviewing and surveying customers on running small experiments and comparing results. The process is meant to be more meritocratic than traditional strategic planning or top-down change models because the data from the surveys and experiments are more objective.

However, lean innovation has a significant problem: even with the best intentions, the prejudices of the executives and teams conducting the experiments overrun the whole process. Surveys and interviews are polluted with bias. Experiments have small sample sizes and no control groups. Running experiments and getting data is not a poor choice. Still, lean innovation presents its conclusions as scientific and objective when, in reality, they are only as good (and sometimes much worse) than bare human intuition. The process ends up being another method of top-down change that elevates the ideas of only a few people who are in charge and ignores countless other potential contributions.

Top-down change—no matter how well-intentioned and well organized—is failing organizations. But there is another way to lead change that enables innovation and change to originate from anyone in an organization, irrespective of their role or authority. As we'll see, the Japanese call this process *nemawashi* or "preparing the roots for change." I call it "piecemeal consensus" or simply "bottom-up change." I stumbled into this novel strategy for leading change ten years ago and, over a decade, experimented with, refined, and proved its effectiveness.

Finally, I simplified what I'd learned into **The Five Steps of Bottom-Up Change** that anyone can follow, and any organization can adopt, to lead change.

The Five Steps of Bottom Up Change

Step 5	Take Deliberate Action
Step 4	Go Over and Up
Step 3	Write A Summary
Step 2	Start with Peers
Step 1	Brainstorm

There is no argument among business leaders that the most successful organizations today are the most innovative. The most innovative organizations must have mechanisms for gathering and elevating the best ideas, no matter who has them. But, in practice, few organizations, whether large for-profit corporations, governments or non-profits, have such a mechanism. Instead, organizations only value and act on the ideas of some people, and ignore the rest.

That's what this book is about: how individuals can advocate effectively for their ideas and how organizations can harness the genius of every single person on their teams. With this book, I intend to suggest one strategy that will fill the gap Mark found in the Apple U curriculum. Piecemeal consensus enables anyone to solve Type II problems they encounter without playing politics.

How this book came about

No idea is entirely new, but the strategy you will read here does challenge many of the common assumptions espoused by classic business books and business schools. While the first step, "Brainstorming," is universal to the point of being a cliché, the other four steps turn traditional strategies for change management and innovations upside down. No matter who you are, whatever your position or role, no matter who you know or where you are on the pay scale, these simple steps will enable you to lead change at your organization.

I discovered this novel way to lead change while I was working as a change management consultant at some of the largest health systems in the US. Health systems are not known for their agility and rapid change. I started to hit multiple dead ends a week with my new ideas. I was getting frustrated and apathetic at work. Out of this frustration, I developed a new strategy for leading change from the bottom up.

I left healthcare, first to become an entrepreneur and then a product manager in San Francisco. While building my businesses and products in Silicon Valley, I further developed and honed the new method of change leadership.

Along the way, I taught my strategy of piecemeal consensus to some of my colleagues. One of my colleagues urged me to write a blog post to explain how it works. When that post helped a few people and gained some popularity, I decided to expand it into this book.

The book is a mixture of practice and theory. Before the end, you will be able to start using this new method to lead change in any organization of which you are a part.

Part I of the book surveys the field of change in organizations by exploring four of the most common strategies organizations embrace when trying to support change and be innovative. These strategies will sound familiar; they include hiring consultants, training management to be open-minded, making the organization "flatter," and building an in-house innovation incubator. While some of these strategies sound great at the outset, we'll see that each is ultimately doomed to fail.

Part II outlines this new bottom-up method for leading change based on the real social dynamics of organizations. It explains how anyone can put the five steps to work immediately, with actual, tangible results.

Part III takes us away from the individual and up to the strategic level. Here, we'll take an insider's look at consistently innovative companies like Amazon, Pixar, and Google. These companies have built sustainable cultures of change leadership by enabling piecemeal consensus. They act as exemplars, providing a route map for how any organization can develop its policies to support its people to establish a culture of innovation.

The stories in this book are real. They will show you how you can successfully lead change, irrespective of if you work in the mailroom or the boardroom of the corporate hierarchy. They will give you a new vocabulary for making change happen. They will provide you with the power of leading change.

PART I

POPULAR APPROACHES TO CHANGE AND THEIR PITFALLS

A successful man will profit from his mistakes and try again in a different way.

DALE CARNEGIE, *HOW TO WIN FRIENDS AND INFLUENCE PEOPLE*

PERMISSION PARALYSIS AND THE CULT OF THE CONSULTANT

When I met Tom, he was 25 years old and working at a successful advertising company in a major city in the Midwest. Let's call the company Turnstyle.

The year after earning an English degree, Tom lived at his mom's house, saved up money, and traveled to Australia for a few months. When he got back to the Midwest, his friend recommended him to Turnstyle, and they hired him. After a few months as a copywriter, he received a promotion to the role of assistant ad buyer.

Tom was good at his job, and his colleagues liked him. Tina, one of the ad buyers he supported, considered him thoughtful and precise. She recommended him for his promotion after less than a year.

Despite working at Turnstyle for only a short time, Tom was loyal. He wasn't restless or very ambitious. He didn't look anxiously towards the horizon like a Disney princess. He liked to contribute. He had gotten his education, traveled the world, and now was starting his career. In short, Tom was a dedicated and mild-mannered employee.

But Tom had one problem at Turnstyle. He had lots and lots of ideas, but felt powerless to make any of his ideas a reality.

He reached out to me to act as a sort of "change therapist." I often play this role for people, and I enjoy it. It means hearing many exciting stories, problems, and drinking good coffee, tea, and beer. I agreed to meet.

Tom was bursting with ideas for Turnstyle. They could be using analytics much better across the board. Bias was polluting Turnstyle's hiring process: interviewers were influencing each other between interviews by inflating or discounting candidates' abilities. This was leading to less consistent and lower quality hiring. The company was spreading itself too thin. They were going after large- and medium-sized clients at the same time and not doing a great job of serving either.

"If we focused on just one segment of the market, we could dominate the region," Tom said. He stared down at the bar, searching in the water stains for a way to communicate all his ideas to the higher-ups at Turnstyle.

When a smart, creative person doesn't know how to lead change, they can feel frustrated or angry, and they might drag their feet or be testy or moody. If their new ideas are not being heard, their eagerness and engagement may begin to flag. They will become skeptical, disengaged, and finally, apathetic. If they stop believing they can make any change, work loses much of its meaning. They might either quit or look for meaning somewhere else in their lives. Tom was not yet apathetic, but his creative energy was flagging.

Tom's ideas sounded great. They might not all turn out to work or be right, but they were excellent hunches and deserved a few experiments to test them. I asked Tom what he had done to get these changes started at Turnstyle. Had he talked to his manager? Maybe he ought to initiate change by going to his boss? That is the most natural solution, isn't it? Bosses today either already are or know they should be open to new ideas, and invite their reports to treat them as a sounding board and a coach for innovation. Shouldn't they?

Tom looked at me and shook his head. His manager was not open to new ideas. His boss kept Tom focused on his immediate deliverables and the happiness of the ad buyers. She was not interested in Tom's "what if" sorts of ideas concerning the company's client strategy or new analytics engines.

"But it's not her fault," Tom explained. The company had ambitious goals, and the ad buyers were stressed and overworked trying to meet them. That meant their assistants, like Tom, were also stressed and overworked. From his manager's perspective, all that only got worse if an assistant had his head in the clouds.

"There isn't really anything I can do anyways. Change comes from way above me," Tom said.

Strategic planning and top-down change

Like at most companies today, change at Turnstyle came from the top down through a process called **Strategic Planning**.

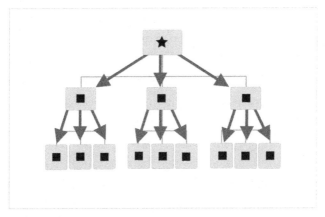

Strategic Planning is the most common strategy for change. In it, new ideas originate at or near the top and then come down through the management hierarchy.

Every quarter or two, members of the C-suite and the VPs went to a lake house or a ski lodge for an offsite strategy meeting. Over strong coffee in the morning and strong drinks at night, they gave presentations, conducted brainstorms, and attempted to make a plan for the business for the next one-to-three years. Upon returning to Turnstyle, the CEO gave a presentation to the whole company outlining the new goals, and the VPs set new metrics and timelines for their departments. People inside the departments would conduct Operational Planning, meaning they would create plans for how to achieve the changes set in strategic planning.

To influence this process, Tom would have to find a way to get his manager to sweet-talk one of the VPs. He didn't hold much hope of that ever happening. Tom admitted he wasn't good at office politics or being an "influencer," and he didn't want to be. Shouldn't common sense be enough? Why did Tom have to play games, be insincere, or stab his colleagues in the back to make change?

"So basically, I'm screwed," Tom concluded and took a sip from his beer.

Strategic planning is the most common strategy for organizational change. The common belief is that change flows from the top down from executives or the outside in from consultants. Business schools reinforce the belief by training tens of thousands of executives and consultants every year in top-down business plans, financial models, and hundred-slide PowerPoint presentations. But this most common of approaches to managing change misses the fact that change can also be led from the bottom up and the inside out.

Strategic planning is the default strategy for change for two very seductive reasons. Those at the top of an organization have an obligation to set the course for the organization, and the position at the top gives them a superior vantage point to view the company than others closer to the front lines. And while these two reasons are certainly true and well-intentioned, top-down change through traditional strategic planning has one enormous unwanted and unintended negative consequence: **permission paralysis**.

Permission paralysis

Permission paralysis happens when change only comes from the top down. The symptoms of this organizational disease are lower engagement, lower productivity, and frustrated team members. People feel that they would be punished for making a change or improvement. Everyone has to wait for permission from above to do anything. They wonder when, finally, they will be allowed to try something new, but the day never comes.

Tom was a poster child for permission paralysis. If only he could get a green light on one of his ideas. Then he could make a real difference. But, as time went on, his hope was evaporating. Turnstyle's permission paralysis was leading Tom into frustration, anger, and resentment. Finally, he would give up on making any changes, or he would quit.

Top-down change causes permission paralysis because the only way for team members to protest a change they disagree with is to drag their feet. When change comes down from the top, it meets a mixed response. Middle-managers and front-line employees either support it, will submit to it, or disagree with it. Since they had no power to influence the change before it happened and now to disagree would mean insubordination, the only possible protest is to slow down their efforts and work to a minimum.

Permission paralysis is a complicated problem to solve. It afflicts some people more than others and can be endemic to the culture of an entire organization. It is a double bind, a Catch-22. It is hard for a single person, no matter what their role is, to cure a culture of permission paralysis. But if everyone waits for permission to make a change, an organization will fossilize in its current state.

Tom felt that if he went ahead and made changes, he would be risking his job and career. At the same time, Tom's managers were under so much pressure that they weren't about to tell Tom to do whatever he wanted with his time.

Tom's story does not have a happy ending. The CEO didn't get wind of Tom's great ideas and promote him. Tom never succeeded in convincing anyone at Turnstyle of anything. Tom clocked in, did his job with care and precision, and kept his superiors happy and his innovative mouth shut. The company staggered from client to client, not failing, but not succeeding in the way Tom knew was possible.

One day, during a company meeting, the CEO made an announcement. Turnstyle was hiring a leading consulting company. Tom was excited. Things would get better, he thought. And they did. Three months and $300,000 later, the consultants presented their report with a series of recommendations. Of the four, two were ideas that Tom had told me over beers more than a year before. People at the company were so excited and grateful, they threw a party for the consultants in appreciation.

Turnstyle's story of strategic planning and hiring consultants is a depressingly familiar solution to the problem of change. Consultants can feel like a shortcut because they can act outside an organization's culture, offering a less disruptive way to harvest and marshal new ideas. But they come at a steep price, both financially and in the form of missed opportunities for improvement and engagement. And, all too often, their proposals result in lackluster success.

Tom was a humble guy. He didn't mind that his company would spend multiples of his annual salary for ideas he had had for more than a year. But it's interesting to ponder an alternative approach. How could Tom have led change on his own? How could Turnstyle have built a culture that would have unfrozen Tom's permission paralysis?

What about Tom's manager? She wasn't helpful at all. And the CEO micromanaging? Isn't that the real problem?

Tom's manager, VPs and CEO weren't open to Tom's new ideas and shut him down. If Tom's manager, VPs and CEO had been more open-minded, maybe Tom's ideas would have had a much better chance of success. To understand if open-minded managers are the solution to change, let's look at another case of a budding change leader, whose managers were more open-minded to change.

2

THE LIMITS OF OPEN-MINDED MANAGEMENT

A wise product manager named Eduardo once told me: "The neck of the bottle is always at the top." Managers, Eduardo explained, are often responsible for narrowing and focusing the energies of a team, but they are also often responsible for putting the kibosh on change. Knowing this, when Eduardo manages a team, he makes a deliberate effort not to micromanage his people and not to be the bottleneck of change. He wants to be open to innovation, information, and ideas.

Tom's manager was the bottleneck. Or was it the micromanaging CEO? Was the only solution for Tom a more open-minded manager, like my friend Eduardo, and a CEO who didn't micromanage the company?

We are bumping into the natural paradox inside every organization: the paradox between running the organization and improving it. Improving an organization and running it compete for resources and time. An organization has to work for its customers and shareholders, and, at the same time, history is littered with the names of defunct organizations that did not change and innovate over time.

One common solution to this paradox is for management to be

more open-minded. If we train our front-line managers to be Eduardos, the story goes, that will make the culture more innovative. Managers should be the ones to balance the paradox of change inside or organizations. Or should they?

To understand this paradox better, let's look at my friend Molly's plan to make a change.

Molly the CSR czar

Molly was working as a mid-level HR manager at a major consulting company in San Francisco. She was concerned about the worsening climate crisis and decided to try to do something about it at work. After some research, Molly found that companies like Apple, Disney, Google, Verizon, AT&T, and Medtronic were creating offices of Corporate Social Responsibility (CSR) with some noteworthy success. She decided to try to start one at her company.

Molly became passionate about all things CSR and could talk for an hour straight about the topic without taking a single breath. She followed all the CSR leaders on Twitter and read everything there was on the internet about the topic. She learned all the do's and don'ts and ins and outs of running one.

Instinctively, though, Molly felt that people at her workplace would not be open to the idea. So, oddly, the more Molly learned and the more her passion grew, the more secretive she became about the idea at work. Molly felt like a double agent. She would glare at the trash bins that did not prompt users to separate their trash. She stifled sighs when she saw catered food wasted. She kept a secret document of all her ideas that the CSR could accomplish, if only. If only.

Molly had the same naïve idea as Tom, and that is very common with potential leaders of change. She thought she had to convince her manager, so her manager would go and convince higher-ups. A process that might look something like this:

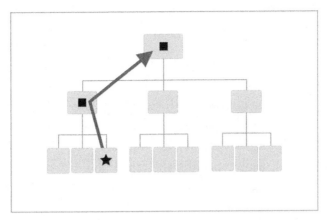

We expect good ideas and changes to go up the hierarchy just like an issue or update does. But they rarely do.

Molly decided that the first thing she needed was to get permission and a budget from her manager. She spent weeks constructing the right way to pitch her idea so that it would appeal to environmentalists and non-environmentalists alike, proving that CSR would be good for the bottom line. She would explain how CSR programs helped leading companies save millions of dollars, retain top talent, and increase brand value while supporting a sustainable planet.

Molly took asking her manager's permission extremely seriously and approached the task with focus and precision. She practiced her pitch and got it down to a tight five minutes and practiced it until it sounded nonchalant. When the time finally came, Molly crossed her fingers, said a little prayer, and went for it.

Molly's manager's name was June. June was open-minded to change and genuinely wanted to see Molly succeed. Open-minded managers don't want to put their reports down and say "No" or "Stay in your lane." Instead open-minded managers use strategies to gently fold innovators back into doing the work they've been assigned to do.

Strategy #1: We Already Tried That

Right out of the gate, June used the tried-and-true "We Already Tried That" strategy.

June praised the idea of a CSR and Molly's intentions. She shook her head sadly. She warned Molly that two years ago, someone had tried to get everyone to print on both sides, and it did not go over well. June didn't want Molly to suffer the same fate. Although Molly felt she had prepared for everything, she hadn't prepared for this response.

But Molly persisted. She made it clear that she would go by the book and not overturn any apple carts or rock any boats.

Strategy #2: We Have Too Much Else To Do

June sighed and switched gears to another strategy for reigning in her report: We Have Too Much Else to Do.

It was right before the new year, so they were slammed with seasonal work before the holidays. In the new year, they had to keep their focus on the spring hires. Molly would have to put her idea for a CSR on the back burner until she had time.

There will always be something going on that prevents us from a change, so claiming not to have the time will always be an honest and effective way to say "Yes," but mean "No." If a boss gives this explanation too many times, of course, it becomes clear that there is never going to be a good time.

Strategy #3: The Encouragement Death Spiral

Molly suggested that she could do the CSR with extra time after work, before work, and even on the weekends. With this offer, June relented for a moment then switched to one of the most subtle killers of change in companies: the Encouragement Death Spiral, also called being Yessed to Death.

On the surface, managers appear to be saying "Yes" to an idea. They are encouraging you to take action. However, along with that encouragement comes an unending list of plausible-sounding requirements. For example:

- The project must have a fully-fledged budget and five-year projections.
- You must first gather baseline values for fifteen success metrics (because we are a data-driven company, of course).
- The project needs a fully built-out maintenance plan for after it succeeds.
- Your manager must sign off on you spending any time on it.
- Your manager's manager needs to sign off on the whole thing.
- Such-and-such committee needs to sign off on it.
- Etc.

Each of these requirements sounds reasonable, but, together, will choke any project to death. So many nit-picky and onerous requirements mean death by a thousand cuts for a fledgling project.

Now, it is easy to say June was not, in fact, that open-minded. Wasn't June acting passive-aggressively or being manipulative? But what if we give June the benefit of the doubt for a moment and look at Molly's request from June's perspective?

The impossible job of front-line managers

Even open-minded managers have the difficult task of prioritizing and executing an organization's business plan. Managers are often under a lot of pressure and have limited resources to complete deliverables on time and hit ambitious metrics. Managers see every task they assign to reports as critical to the success of the team and the company. A new idea or change takes their reports' time away from that work. Some new ideas are in direct conflict with existing priorities. It is an essential part of any manager's job to keep employees on track doing the work assigned for them to do.

Managers do the hard work of maintaining the status quo. That might not sound like something to brag about, but remember that the status quo today was the innovation of the past. Someone needs to keep the wheels from falling off. Someone must execute the business plan as it is written today. Managers are incentivized to be conservative agents in a company, but many companies say, "Go to your manager with new ideas." Is it fair or realistic to expect managers to be both conservative and innovative at the same time?

Front-line managers are, almost by definition, the most numerous and least experienced managers in the company. They have limited time, teams, and resources. Is it reasonable to ask them to use some of their precious resources to invent and experiment with new ideas? Can front-line managers be both obedient soldiers who execute the strategy handed down to them from executives, and creative renegades responsible for conducting experiments and making change? It's not realistic; nevertheless, most people's first thought and many companies' policy for new ideas is to take them to front-line managers.

What if Molly, and all of us, are making a mistake when we take new ideas to our managers? Where else could Molly go?

The paradox of change

Hierarchical organizations are efficient at executing a single elaborate plan. That's why we structure almost all organizations as hierarchies. Through escalations from their reports, managers can collect, synthesize, and distribute information efficiently. They can also, simultaneously, keep track of each of its parts and make sure they are all going along with the broader strategy. It is a miracle when you stop and appreciate it.

Hierarchies achieve this wonder by moving certain kinds of information up and down an organization efficiently. Goals and orders come down from above, and metrics and escalations come from below.

When we go to our manager with a new idea or improvement, we're treating a new idea for change as if it were an issue that needed escalating up the managerial hierarchy. This is a mistake. New ideas for change are not issues that require escalation. New ideas do not move efficiently up a hierarchy the way escalations do.

Here lies the crux of the problem: it is efficient to manage organizations with hierarchies, but hierarchies resist change. Ideally, we'd be able to manage a company from the top down as an efficient hierarchy and at the same time, get well-formed new ideas for change from anywhere in the company. But that's a paradox of change that organizations struggle to overcome. It takes an intentional change in culture, a special mechanism, to overcome these two contradictory forces.

Training managers to be open-minded is the most common solution to the paradox of change, because it suggests a cure for a hierarchy's shortcomings when it comes to change. But it is unrealistic to ask managers to take on the contradictory roles of efficient manager and steward of innovation. The incentives and real dynamics of a company will make managers value efficiency over trying something new.

So, is another approach to solving this paradox to doubt its first premise? If hierarchies naturally resist change, why don't we eliminate the hierarchy altogether? The flatter the organization, the better, yes?

Moving beyond David and Goliath

Molly, like many innovators, framed her battle to start a CSR policy as a David and Goliath story. She was a scrappy David, and the gatekeeper in her way was a hulking Goliath. She was looking for the right stone and sling to knock him out. This framing of change makes the underdog the hero of the story, which they are, but it also makes them the victim of the story, unless they can somehow topple the great giant.

A "Me vs. Them" narrative is counterproductive, and leading change does not need to be as confrontational as the old biblical story. Creating confrontational situations with managers or imagining your victory against a faceless corporation is often self-deception and a waste of energy.

As we'll see in Part II, with a less confrontational and bottom-up strategy for leading change, Molly could use a fraction of the energy she spent preparing her pitch and researching, and already have made the CSR a reality.

3

FALLING FLAT

When I met Brooke, she was spinning her wheels at a hundred miles per hour, trying to make change at her company. The only problem: her wheels weren't on the ground.

Brooke worked at a large company that produced automotive chemical products. Brooke was a trained biochemist with over a decade of experience in advanced technical and chemical manufacturing techniques. Her career started in Detroit, and her most prominent clients were the Big Three automotive companies: Ford, Chrysler, and GM.

"But then Tesla happened," she said. Tesla showed entrepreneurs that they could innovate inside the multi-billion-dollar automotive market. Electric cars required a different set of tolerances and properties, and startups, many of which were based in California, set out to fill the gaps. Some startups started making car parts, and others began making whole new cars and motorcycles.

This jolt of new competition jumpstarted the old automotive companies. Chevrolet, Ford, Nissan, Audi, and Mercedes all started making new products like electric cars and experimenting with new business models. Jaguar, who only made cars, started selling parts.

Brooke volunteered to move out to San Francisco and help her company get involved in this new startup automotive market. When she arrived in San Francisco, she started building relationships with new parts and vehicle manufacturers. It became clear that her company was being left in the dust and would need to make rapid changes back in Detroit to keep up. The problem was that Detroit wasn't listening to Brooke.

Brooke's first strategy was to marshal as much data as possible to support her position. Being a trained scientist surrounded by scientists and engineers, she thought that data would convince her colleagues. Her cold hard facts, models, and projections would prove that her radical ideas for change were necessary. No such luck. They kept telling her, "It's different in Detroit."

When Brooke had moved to San Francisco, she read *The Lean Startup*. The book set her heart on fire for running experiments and making change. Unfortunately, her colleagues were not as hip to the lean startup buzz as she was. The harder she argued and pushed for more iterative experimentation behavior, the more they dug in their heels.

To Brooke, her colleagues were making no sense. Why were these engineers and scientists not listening to the data she presented? Why were they fighting iterative experimentation?

Brooke's lucky break

Brooke decided that she must be talking to the wrong people. If she could pitch her ideas to those at the absolute top of the company, those with the real power, she could have an impact. Almost by sheer luck, Brooke's dream came true.

Occasionally at Brooke's company, someone gets the chance to give a presentation to a panel of senior VPs and a member of the C-suite about what they are working on. Right when Brooke was about to throw in the towel, she was chosen to give one of these coveted presentations.

This was it, Brook thought. She had been given a chance every innovator would die for. She would have a room full of executives and a Chief of Something Officer all in one place with only one purpose: to listen to her great ideas. And Brooke was not going to waste the opportunity.

She loaded up a slide deck to explain how different the market and customers were in San Francisco and the risks this posed to Detroit. She proposed a broad, three-point plan to adapt and lead in this evolving marketplace. She gave the presentation and nailed it.

The feedback she got from the panel made her heart sink into her shoes. Brooke expected in-depth follow-up questions, requests for more information, or at least compelling objections. Instead, the feedback was on the level of a high school public speaking course. "You could say fewer filler words like 'um,' and 'uh,'" one read. "Some of your slides were wordy and hard to follow," read another. At that moment, Brooke was closer than ever to quitting her job.

As Brooke saw the evidence mounting in favor of her ideas, her company's opposition to them only increased. It didn't make sense. Brooke concluded that her company was just too bureaucratic.

Down with bureaucracy!

Brooke saw bureaucracy as the real culprit for why she couldn't make any change at her company.

The way things looked to Brooke, the more levels of management there are between a CEO and a front-line employee, the less agile and innovative a company will be. The flatter an organization is—the fewer levels of management it has—the lighter an organization is on its toes, and the easier it will be to innovate and make changes. Until they eliminated some layers of management, making change felt hopeless.

From *Dilbert* comics to the show *The Office*, we blame bureaucracy for stifling new ideas and change. And that's understandable; we've all sat across from a smiling gatekeeper telling you "No." If we could eliminate bureaucracy, or reduce its influence as much as possible, we would unblock all the innovators those bureaucrats are stopping in their tracks. Wouldn't we?

In Tom's case at Turnstyle, his closed-minded manager and micro-managing CEO stifled change. And in Molly's case, even her open-minded manager had a chilling effect on Molly's idea for an office of CSR. Do hierarchies necessarily stifle innovation? Will flatter organizations always be better at change?

Meet holocracy

Let's look at three companies that all tore down their hierarchies and established ultra-flat organizational structures, each with varying degrees of success.

1. Zappos, an e-commerce shoe app
2. Valve, a top-tier video game software company
3. Medium.com, a popular long-form blogging website

Each of these companies was led by charismatic, visionary CEOs that eliminated the management hierarchy and adopted a flat organizational philosophy called holocracy.

The term holocracy was coined in 2007 by a software engineer CEO named Brian Robertson when he published the "Holocracy Constitution." He went on to establish a consulting company that helps organizations adopt holocratic governance.

Holocracy eliminates the role of "boss." Employees manage themselves. Each person decides what they think is essential to work on and what team to join. Since anyone can work on anything, individual employees can start working on tasks, and if other people join them, this forms a new "circle" or autonomous team.

Circles set goals democratically and elect some of their members the job of communicating with other circles to streamline inter-circle communication. Each circle's goals are the boss of that circle. The members of the circle enforce the goals as a group. The members of the circle hold each other accountable. If the circle starts falling behind, the team rallies each other with encouragement and warnings of what the consequences will be if they don't meet their goal. During many circle "governance meetings," participants set and update these metrics. The whole company itself represents the largest circle. Company-wide goals are set at company town hall meetings or smaller "governance meetings" of elected representatives from other circles.

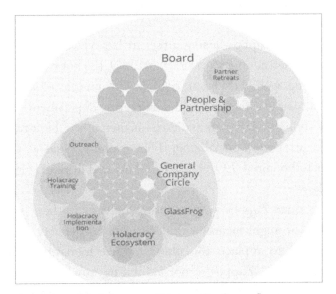

An org chart of the holocracy at Holocracy One Source: Image courtesy of HolocracyOne

The entire structure is fluid. Anyone can leave a circle or join another circle. Anyone can work wherever they want or wherever they believe the company has needs, and that circle will accept them. If the organization is more flexible, proponents suggest, it will be more innovative and more responsive to change. All of this will lead to higher productivity, significant innovation, and, hopefully, substantial profits.

However, there were few visible benefits to switching to holocracy for the billion-dollar online shoe app Zappos.

The case of Zappos

Tony Hsieh, the CEO of Zappos, led the company to adopt holocracy in 2014, but not without a fight. There was substantial pushback, which led to twenty percent of the company taking the severance deal Hseih offered to the most significant anti-holocracy nay-sayers. Hsieh and his true believers were free to conduct their organizational experiments.

I visited the Zappos headquarters in Las Vegas, Nevada, a few months after they adopted holocracy. At HQ, the holocracy appeared to be working well. Hsieh sat right in the middle of a cluttered, colorful bullpen of cubes inside the marketing department. In classic holocracy style, the CEO didn't have his own office. Holocracy even influenced after-work socializing. That evening, I sat at the same table as its billionaire CEO, eating Pad Thai and drinking ginger beer and whiskey.

At the time Zappos was adopting holocracy, there was buzz around what it might mean for the company and society as a whole: are we ready to replace the old-fashioned hierarchy? However, several years later, Zappos is not exhibiting any visible holocratic benefits. There have been no significant technological innovations or financial windfalls to support its expensive switch to holocracy. By some embarrassingly public metrics, Zappos has become a worse place to work since adopting holocracy.

In 2009, before adopting holocracy, Zappos boasted being ranked twenty-third out of Forbes 100 Best Places to Work. Two years after selecting holocracy and parting ways with the three hundred most dissatisfied employees in the company, Zappos slipped to eighty-fourth out of Forbes the same list—surpassed by sixty-one organizations that were not holocracies.

It is hard to estimate Zappos's financial success as a holocracy because it is a part of Amazon. The best evidence against its shift to a flat structure is the complete lack of news about it. In the years of operating with the purest of pure holocracies, it appears nothing remarkable has happened there. Zappos continues to sell shoes online, but the benefits of its costly move to holocracy are far from clear.

The case of Valve

The billion-dollar gaming company, Valve, has also adopted holocracy. At Valve, there was some evidence that switching their culture has helped them stay on the bleeding edge of one of the fastest moving industries in the world.

Valve was a total holocracy, so much so that the company was famous for employees voting to set each other's salaries. Valve employees could work on whatever they found interesting. Since everyone was interested in video games, they crowded around and worked on the games they thought were the best.

Holocracy was working well for Valve. It turns out video game engineers are the best judges of video games and video game technology. At traditional gaming companies, game titles might be the brainchild of a founder or executive or have originated with marketing team focus groups, and then forced onto the engineers to build. But Valve's employees were some of the most hardcore and most critical gamers in existence. It made sense to let them swarm around anything that they found fascinating—project, game, or otherwise.

Valve's game franchises were consistently hits, many with millions of players worldwide. It was unique as a game studio since it created blockbuster games like *Counter-Strike* alongside indie game sensations like *Portal* (2007) and *Portal 2* (2011). Also, one of Valve's most significant successes was not a game at all, but a game downloading platform called Steam, released in 2003.

Holocracy was working brilliantly for a company that revolutionized the entire industry of video games more than once in its twenty-plus-year history, but it was not a perfect system. In July 2018, PCgamer.com reported that one ex-Valve employee described working at Valve as a complex web of internal politics, backstabbing, and manipulation. Employees were doing everything they could within the system to secure bonuses, promotions, and their jobs. Holocracy had the significant drawback of making playing office politics a requirement for every employee.

Valve reaped the benefits of chaotic creativity that holocracy affords, and those benefits outweighed the stress of cutthroat office politics. But not every organization needs to produce hit video games every few years. And when an organization does not benefit from so much chaotic creativity, holocracy itself can buckle. For example, look to the case of Medium.com's failed experiment with holocracy.

The case of Medium.com

The CEO of Medium, Evan Williams, was one of holocracy's most prominent evangelists. In 2013, right about the time that Hsieh was signing severance checks, the upstart internet publisher Medium adopted the purest of pure holocracies. Yet by 2016, it dropped holocracy after a rocky three-year experiment.

In a postmortem blog post, Williams explained what happened. While Medium still wanted to embrace a flat organizational structure, he wrote, an obsession with holocracy processes were getting in the way of doing actual work. The necessary circle governance meetings were wasting too much time. The internal politics that holocracy necessitated was slowing real work to a crawl.

Many holocracy evangelists believed that holocracy would work best in small organizations, but Medium had only ninety employees and was flagging. For an example of an even smaller company, there was Hapi, a software company with only thirty employees. After a year with holocracy in 2017, the CEO went on record as saying that the structure led to "too many chiefs, not enough Indians." Like at

Medium, there were too many people doing decision making and not enough people doing the work.

At first, holocracy looks like a lighter burden than the bureaucracy of a hierarchy. But in practice, in a holocracy, the number and length of meetings explodes. When a company throws out their hierarchy, they still have to develop an intricate operational plan and stay accountable to that plan. Since there are no bosses or management, making decisions means persuading people in crushingly long democratic "circle governance meetings." As Medium's story illustrates, all the extra meetings and processes add considerable overhead to even a small company.

Medium ditched holocracy, but still wanted to be as flat as possible. But after looking at the extreme flatness of holocracy, should we continue to see organizational flatness as a panacea for accelerating change and improving innovation?

While organizational hierarchies might benefit from some deep pruning, organizational flatness is no silver bullet for making an organization lighter on its toes. While an efficient org chart helps, flatness on its own won't make a company innovative. Nor does a few layers of bureaucracy always spell disaster for change.

There is also an upside to a manageable amount of bureaucracy. Managers keep a business running day-to-day. Some organizations have more middle management because they need to train large numbers of entry-level employees, monitor their performance, and handle frequent escalations. And a management hierarchy, oddly enough, actually reduces the lengths and number of meetings that would be necessary for its absence.

So, can an organizations enjoy both the efficiencies of a hierarchy and unlock the creativity of every teammate? I believe the answer is "Yes," if individuals use piecemeal consensus and organizations adopt a strategy of bottom-up change and innovation.

Whatever the answer, these stories of holocracy suggest that the solution is not as easy as firing all the bosses.

4

THE IN-HOUSE INCUBATOR

So far, we've looked at three frequent attempts to resolve the inherent tension between executing a business model efficiently as it is, and changing or improving it. Having no strategy for change leads to permission paralysis. The policy of training open-minded managers backfires since the primary role of managers is to execute a business strategy as it is, not to change it. Eliminating or flattening an organization's hierarchical structure has substantial costs and can result in a lack of direction, long meetings, and rampant office politics.

Let's look at a fourth standard and, currently, the mainstream strategy for enabling change in an organization: in-house incubators.

Y Combinator or "YC" is the most famous startup incubator in the world. Their headquarters are located in the bellybutton of Silicon Valley in Palo Alto, California. Their lobby has toothy, orange plastic walls and low grey couches like the interior decoration out of a sci-fi movie from the late 90s.

Incubators like Y Combinator are programs that take in young, unformed, and unproven startups and cultivate them until they become full-fledged companies.

Y Combinator is responsible for finding and helping billion-dollar "unicorn" companies to start, such as Airbnb, Stripe, Cruise, Dropbox, Coinbase, Instacart, and others.

Incubators like YC and their peers, TechStars and 500Startups, have inspired corporate innovation teams to build their own internal incubators. Large corporations took their cue from the startup buzz happening outside their organizations. And now, internal incubation has become the state-of-the-art strategy for corporate innovation. Many business classics outline the blueprints for the internal incubator, including Steve Blank's *The Four Steps to the Epiphany*, or *The Startup Way* by Eric Ries, the author of *The Lean Startup*. These books prescribe a change playbook that focuses on discovering, validating, and growing new ideas inside organizations—but away from day-to-day business operations.

Combining the benefits of traditional—and efficient—working structures and processes with the cultures of proven tech incubators might look like a win-win. However, in 2010, a Fortune 500 company invited me and my team to help them develop an internal incubation program, and I learned firsthand the inherent problems it can bring.

Phase 1: Discovery

On the first day of the project, we drove way out to the suburbs and parked in the ocean of a parking lot. We made our way into one of the two-story, khaki stucco and green glass office buildings. We walked through dimly lit hallways flanked by cubicles with floors covered in grey-purple industrial carpeting and low ceilings made of plasterboard panels and fluorescent lights.

Once we reached the offices of the innovation team, everything changed.

The innovation offices were well lit. There were no cubicles. The walls were painted the same warm, dark orange as Y Combinator's lobby, and the floor had a sizable, shaggy, lime green rug. On one side of the room was an L-shaped couch and bean bags that faced a large flatscreen TV. Littered around the TV were an Xbox and its controllers and games. In bookshelves next to the TV, there were Japanese and American action figures and collectibles, mind teaser puzzles, board games, small robots and electronic knickknacks. On the other side of the room, the walls were covered edge-to-edge with whiteboards. There were low-backed white chairs with wheels on their feet around a modular white table. The table could snap into a breakout configuration of four separate tables at a moment's notice. Up against the other wall, I noticed a six-armed drone and its controller. Next to the drone stood a gleaming, chrome unicycle.

Our client had invited us to help them develop a Y Combinator-esque internal incubator. The goal was to find, prove, and grow new ideas that would someday contribute to their company's bottom line.

In standard consultant fashion, we dedicated our first meeting to learning more about their organization and their goals. We started with a free-form conversation about their organization to determine what the success of an internal incubator meant for them. We were beginning to understand how many competing interests this innovation team was up against. It might be impossible for them to maneuver at all.

The team was hoping that the incubator would create a sort of innovation superhighway that could get ideas out of the gnarled jungle of day-to-day, quarter-to-quarter pressures. The more we learned, the more we were convinced that their organization would never allow a new program like the incubator to exist with any semblance of independence. Nevertheless, we were eager for a challenge, so we agreed to try.

After a month of preparation, we sat down again with the innovation team to make our recommendation.

Phase 2: The Recommendation

Many of the startups that got into Y Combinator (or attempted to) were following the teachings of one man: Eric Ries and his revolutionary book *The Lean Startup*. Ries contributed to the tidal wave of tech startups by chronicling the process of developing a tech startup and teaching it to an ocean of budding entrepreneurs.

Ries observed that there were parallels between lean manufacturing and tech startups. Lean manufacturing was inspired by the business culture of Toyota, as described by Taiichi Ohno in his 1978 book *Toyota Production System*. In *The Lean Startup*, Ries adapted two of the many key Toyota manufacturing concepts and applied them to tech startups: *kaizen* or "continual improvement" (what Ries calls "iteration") and *kaikaku* or "radical change," (what Ries calls "a pivot"). You don't have to have binge-watched the popular HBO series *Silicon Valley* to recognize that the words "iteration" and "pivot" have now entered into our mainstream language. Ries's book is, in large part, responsible for the popularization of these ideas both in tech and our society at large.

Ries promised his readers that, as long as they continued to iterate and pivot, their success was inevitable. In practice, Ries's advice may be an oversimplification, but many people followed it, learned a great deal, and some found success.

Soon after Ries's ideas swept the world of tech entrepreneurship, large companies asked Ries to help them manage corporate change and innovate. Ries spent the next five years consulting with large corporations about innovation. His work with large companies became the basis for his second book, *The Startup Way*. *The Startup Way* was a manual for how companies can use the methodology of *The Lean Startup* internally.

My team and I were developing an internal incubator about five years before *The Startup Way* hit the shelves. We had our well-thumbed copies of *The Lean Startup* to rely on, and we went about building an in-house incubator roughly the same way Ries would recommend. Over the ensuing months, we were able to teach the client about incubation and help them develop a plan for their new incubation program.

Incubating ideas inside a company has four steps analogous to the stages of developing a tech startup:

1. **Discover** a good idea
2. **Validate** that the idea will succeed
3. **Iterate** on the idea to improve it
4. **Scale** the idea up

Innovation officers know that there are lots of ideas popping up all over an organization all the time. Good ideas will lead to value for the company. Bad ones might turn into boondoggles. The challenge of the first phase is to discern between these two.

Pfizer, a multinational pharmaceutical company with approximately 94,000 employees, uses a digital idea "stock market" to pick some of the ideas they incubate. Employees put their proposals on the exchange. All employees receive an allowance of digital money they can use to buy shares of the ideas they think will succeed. The prices of those ideas go up, signaling to executives and innovation officers to start to validate and grow them. If an idea achieves some success, the price goes up even more, and the employees who bought the stock early on can sell the stock for a cash bonus.

We recommended a more straightforward solution. The innovation team would develop a rubric to assess ideas with such categories as Revenue Potential, Ease of Implementation, Operational Alignment, etc. They could incubate the ideas that score above a certain threshold on that rubric. We got nods all around. Maybe this internal incubator would work after all.

Inspired by Y Combinator's success, we recommended a twelve-week intensive incubator. The curriculum of the program centered on the innovation team setting up each candidate in the program with close mentorship from volunteering company executives. The candidates ought to be exempted from their regular jobs to pursue building their idea. The first phase would be rapid-paced mentor speed dating, followed by weekly check-ins with the matching mentors and the innovation team. Each candidate would document any significant learnings and pivots in reports that were turned in each week to the innovation team to review. At the end of twelve weeks, there would be a demo day, where the participants would develop a deck to attract excitement and support from executives and leadership for their idea.

Phase 3: The Incubator's Constraints

In the middle of our presentation, the innovation team members' smiles started turning into winces.

They loved our recommendation, but there were significant problems they saw. They could not pry incubator participants away from their divisions, teams, and managers for twelve weeks. Participants could devote no more than five hours per week to work on their projects and would be in the program for as short a time as possible.

Executives, we learned, would not help participants create new projects since these new projects could threaten the teams, products, and budgets they already managed. Mentorship would be limited; only the innovation team (a total of five people) would serve as mentors. While supportive and sharp, the innovation team did not know the ins and outs of the company's complex products and structure.

There could be no demo day. The executive team had decided it would be unwise to give the participants in the incubator a high profile. They worried that elevating some people in this way would create a sense of unfair treatment between the incubator participants and their corporate peers and managers.

Lastly, they could not promise the participants that they would be allowed to stay with their idea. Executives would move successful projects into new divisions. Personnel were not permitted to change divisions without being rehired for an open position in that division. So, there was a real danger that a participant, having developed the original idea, would not be allowed to continue to work on their project.

If a project were to survive and thrive despite all of these limitations, there was an additional constraint. Any executive who liked a new idea might vie to take it over or kill it, and in all likelihood, they would succeed.

The innovation team was setting up an incubation program that had multiple fatal flaws. It was going to be a program that gave its participants hope but also withheld the time and support they would need to ever succeed. Who would risk entering a program where they were likely to fail? And after a dozen failures, who would continue funding the team and time needed to run this incubator?

The challenges internal incubators face

Were these constraints unique to this one client's organization, or were they going to turn up again and again in every traditional company? This client was an old company with a traditional culture and an entrenched bureaucracy. Surely not all big companies and no young and small-to-medium size companies were like this?

After working with more companies on their incubators, it became clear that our first client was not unique. Internal incubators were facing some version of the same problems, no matter what the size and age of the company was.

Companies, especially large companies, are attracted to the incubation model of innovation because it promises to be a system of change that works alongside the hierarchical structure of a company. From the outside, an incubation program looks like a highway for change. Good ideas get onto the highway and accelerate over the streets of everyday bureaucracy to their destination.

However, the internal incubation model promises much on paper, but does not deliver as much in practice.

Practically speaking, it is impossible to construct an independent incubator inside a company because everything is connected. Executives howl about inefficiency and defend their turf and budgets everywhere. And who can blame them? Creating and exploring new ideas pulls people, time, and money away from what they see as critical business functions.

So how do we lead change in an organization? And how do we build a culture that supports innovation? If open-minded managers are not the silver bullet, your organization is not going to take the plunge into holocracy, and if it is not feasible nor wise to deploy a compromised incubation program, what else is there? How does one employee lead change, and how does an individual or an organization as a whole lead change?

PART II

THE FIVE STEPS OF BOTTOM-UP CHANGE

Anyone can cook!

AUGUSTE GUSTEAU, *RATATOUILLE*

5

STUMBLING INTO CHANGE

My colleague Nikolai and I discovered the piecemeal consensus strategy for change by accident. We made the discovery over a year-long period as we were leading the development and adoption of a piece of software that became a critical tool for more than 7,000 people.

Nikolai and I met on our first day working at Epic—a quirky, sprawling, 7,000-employee, multi-billion-dollar healthcare software company. Nikolai was charming and a natural salesman. He was also a wiz with a spreadsheet. He had worked for a bank for years during college and climbed their corporate ladder while also earning his Master of Science in economics from Boston University.

Epic hired Nikolai into HR, and within two months, he had built a spreadsheet that automated his and four other people's jobs. The higher-ups identified him as "talent" and made him the assistant to the CTO. In his new role, Nikolai had enormous latitude. Primarily, he took on helping special projects across the company.

At that time, I was flying to both coasts multiple times per month, pulling the sorts of thankless, burn-out sixty- to eighty-hour weeks. My google calendar looked like a plaid shirt. I would pick which overlapping meetings to attend based on which project was most in crisis. I was receiving 250 emails per day. When I wasn't answering emails, writing documents, or making presentations on my laptop, I was leading high stakes phone calls with one customer while sitting in a closet on-site at another.

When I was not traveling, Nikolai and I had 'idea jams' in Nikolai's office. We would shoot back and forth ideas about things we'd learned in the past few weeks. We'd kibitz about what was broken or flawed in the operation of the company around us.

If that all wasn't enough, I was also teaching myself to be a software engineer. I worked through tutorials, and when I came up against problems, I found all my answers on the question and answer website named Stackoverflow.com. Stack Overflow is like a dynamic frequently asked questions platform focused on technical software engineering problems. It's one of the most popular websites on the internet, and many professional software engineers would be lost without it.

In one of these Nikolai jam sessions, I threw out an idea offhandedly.

"If we just had an internal Stack Overflow, it would double the efficiency of our consultants. Maybe we could even make a public one for client questions." Nikolai blinked. I blinked. Nikolai turned to face his computer.

"Maybe more than double," he said. "If we assume there is a ton of repetition in the questions clients ask, and we assume a Stack Overflow system would make everyone ask and answer each question only once...," he trailed off. He turned back to me and pulled one of his ear-to-ear grins. Giggling and smiling maniacally, he said: "We should make it!"

A case of permission paralysis and gatekeeper X

Nikolai and I fell straight into permission paralysis.

The company resources were all behind a wall of area owners, executives, VPs, and managers. We needed permission to use our own time and the time of other folks in the company, and to have access to the servers on the company's internal internet.

I did not yet have the engineering skills to build a Q&A platform for us. We would have to ask for software engineers' help, but it was boom-time for Epic, and engineers' time was scarce.

I asked Nikolai if he could go to his boss, the CTO, and ask him to greenlight the new internal Stack Overflow as a special project. Nikolai shook his head. He knew the CTO would not go for this.

Instead, Nikolai sent up some smoke signals into the engineering team, and right away, a middle-managing engineer flagged us down. Call him Gatekeeper X. He set up a meeting on the calendar in two weeks. We waited for our hearing with the great and terrible Oz. We visited him in his tiny grey office and shared the idea of an internal Stack Overflow.

Gatekeeper X shot straight out with the classic strategy, "We Already Tried That." What we were building already existed, and some engineers were already using it. Sorry.

It didn't bother us that someone had already built the platform. We wanted more people to use it. Could consultants and other teams in the company use the Q&A system?

Gatekeeper X gave us an "atta-boy" for our efforts and launched straight into the **Encouragement Death Spiral**.

It was possible to get more people to use the website, but it wouldn't be easy. In an encouraging tone, Gatekeeper X described to us the intractable and byzantine web of look-overs and sign-offs we needed. The process he explained, I estimate now, would have taken us approximately the rest of our lives.

We left the meeting with Gatekeeper X deflated. For the next few weeks, I started a hard month of travel. I crisscrossed the country sometimes twice per week and worked from 7 a.m. to 9 p.m. on most days. Nikolai spent those weeks ticking off as many of the death spiral demands Gatekeeper X had given us as he could. Nikolai also gave Gatekeeper X's Q&A platform some close inspection. He found it lacked both features and users. It had been cobbled together quickly, fell short in terms of delivery, and was never looked at again.

We had a windfall. I stumbled across a list of ten open source clones of Stack Overflow. I plucked the best looking one off the shelf and spent a few days trying to start the project. Finally, I got it to work, and I showed it to Nikolai. We did a little celebration dance in his office. Finding the open-source project meant we didn't need engineers to build something from scratch. All we needed now was permission to put our little site up on a server with access to Epic's internal internet.

Nikolai asked a few people for permission to put a website up internally and was either shrugged off or turned down. There was no official way to request space on an internal webserver. Only official projects could officially get server space. And since Nikolai's and my plan was not an official project, we could not get server space —officially.

Encouragement and validation from users

As the technical side of things moved in fits and starts, so did the marketing side. Nikolai showed the prototype of our cloned Stack Overflow to one of the lead VPs in the consulting division named Eric. Eric's current software was clunky, and he was bent on finding a better solution. When he found Nikolai and my fledgling project, he became its champion. He let us interview him about consultant work-flows and promised that his team would be the first to adopt our software once it was live.

Eric taught us that most of the essential knowledge in the company was sitting in people's private email inboxes. When you asked a top consultant a question, they often would not know the answer off the top of their head, but they could make a quick search of their inbox to pull up the email that contained the answer. With Eric's feedback, we became more confident that our Q&A platform would be a success if we could ever get it live.

Eric asked us a strange question: why were we doing this? Why were we adding even more work to our already overloaded schedules? Work that no one was asking us to do that both of us were hiding from our managers. Was it our cunning ambition to climb to the top of corporate America? Would we someday reveal our efforts in all their glory?

It wasn't any of that.

We simply liked efficiency. It bothered us when people wasted their time, and when we knew a process could be faster and better. Nikolai automated himself out of his first job in HR. I was sick and tired of answering the same questions over and over again. Efficiency for Nikolai and I, and for many people, was an itch we had to scratch.

But the real reason, I believe now, is because it was fun and challenging to build something people would want to use.

Jeff and his server

Finally, something in our brains broke, and we decided: "No more gatekeepers."

Nikolai put out his feelers to some engineers and found Jeff, a novice web developer. Jeff had started about the same time as Nikolai and I. We told Jeff our idea. He nodded at everything we said and joined our team. We explained our trials and tribulations of trying to ask permission for server space. He understood and nodded again. I showed him the open-source clone I had spun up. He nodded again.

"I have a server under my desk we can use. I was given it to test, but I can connect it to the intranet securely. I can put the code on it tonight, and we'll be live by tomorrow."

Nikolai and I almost cried.

The next day I was updating the colors and administrator settings, preparing for the influx of the first team that would start using the platform. I realized it had no name. Nikolai wanted me to name it since the project had been my idea originally. Everything at Epic was named after celestial bodies. At that time, I had learned about the western shoulder of Orion, a red supergiant star about 642 light-years from earth named Betelgeuse, pronounced *beetlejuice* like the cult movie from the 80's with Michael Keaton.

"Like that weird movie?" Nikolai asked. I shrugged. Nikolai laughed. The name appealed to his sense of the absurd. Betelgeuse it was. He made a monstrosity of a logo, and I loaded it into the site.

I put in a few test questions and answers, and Jeff double-checked that there were no bugs. We were copasetic. The site was live and stable. Nikolai showed the live site to Eric, and Eric agreed to float the idea to other people on his team. After two weeks, thirty of Eric's consultants were using the platform. After a few weeks more, Eric's team had abandoned their old software and embraced the Q&A platform as their knowledge management system.

Slowly but surely, we picked up a few hundred users. After three months, the lead of my division (my boss's boss's boss) presented Betelgeuse to the company. She said it was a new tool that we would all use for knowledge management. I was floored. I was smiling at that meeting. It felt good to see an idea coming into its own and helping my team.

Not all the credit we expected

Although I felt good about Betelgeuse's success, I was also a bit disappointed. Where were the garlands, the prizes, the bonus, the promotion, the raise? I received no standing ovation, no credit. A few people around me nodded and smiled at me, knowing that I was close to the center of the force that moved this project into being. Some of the management knew of my contributions. Nikolai and I had built a system that would save and make millions more for this billion-dollar business. Where was the love?

Building Betelgeuse did help my career. People talked about my hand in the project, and it grew my reputation. If I had stayed longer at Epic, my work on Betelgeuse would have spring-boarded me into application leadership.

I realized what people meant when they say leaders need to be humble. When you lead change, you don't get all the credit. The real payoff for building Betelgeuse was helping people. Epic helped hospitals succeed, and hospitals help people who are sick. By extension, Betelgeuse helped people who needed it. If you work at a company you believe in, and this belief has a positive impact, leading change is a great way to make the world better.

Almost a year after we had started, we had succeeded in our goal. We had launched a new knowledge management platform at a major software company. No manager had asked us to do it; in fact, a few had tried to stop us. But how had we done it?

We had not been fast or efficient—we made every mistake in the book. But could our experience be instructive for other leaders? It took me another decade working as an entrepreneur, leader, and product manager, and over a year of research, to uncover how and why what we did worked. Finally, I cut away all the mistakes we made and boiled the process we followed down to **The Five Steps of Bottom-Up Change**:

The Five Steps of Bottom Up Change

Step 5	Take Deliberate Action
Step 4	Go Over and Up
Step 3	Write A Summary
Step 2	Start with Peers
Step 1	Brainstorm

Along the way, I learned that we had discovered more than just an excellent way to get projects started and move them along. We had found a flaw and a missing link in agile project management itself: a mistranslated and forgotten Japanese concept called *nemawashi*.

6

NEMAWASHI: THE POWER OF PIECEMEAL CONSENSUS

"*Nemawashi* is a bad word," Miki said to me with a conspiratorial air. "What do you want to know about it?"

Miki was my company's country manager in Japan. I was trying to understand what Nikolai and I had done with Betelgeuse at Epic. I went to her when the winding road of research into leading change led me to this strange Japanese word. I was struggling to make sense of it.

"Basically, it means 'to make a deal,'" Miki told me. "You talk, maybe have some drinks, and you make a deal about something else." I nodded, urging her to continue. "Some people have power, but some people actually have power. You go and talk to them, and you make a deal." Miki spread her hands as if that was all there was to say.

Miki was a native speaker of Japanese who spoke excellent, bubbling English, but she did not know how to translate *nemawashi* precisely. It's not her fault. I found out later that the word has no direct translation into English. The word is utterly foreign. It also is the key to leading change at work.

Preparing the roots

The word *nemawashi* comes from the world of Japanese gardening, and is a compound word that means "to prepare the roots."

When a gardener transplants a plant, it undergoes high levels of stress. To reduce the stress, Japanese gardeners bring soil from the destination site and put it around the plant's roots before moving the plant. The plant acclimatizes to its new location before moving, making the transplant safer and easier.

I went back to Miki and told her what I had learned about transplanting plants, and it reminded her of an excellent example of *nemawashi* from the business world.

Miki's friend, Taro Kodama, was the country manager of Facebook in Japan. He was a Japanese American born in Los Angeles, and, in his business career, specialized in cross-cultural Japanese-American businesses and products. He set up a triumphant deal between a major Japanese advertising firm and Facebook that drove adoption of the platform across the country. Miki considered him a master of *nemawashi*, without meaning him any offense, of course.

"He is a specialist in both cultures. He prepared both sides, had drinks, went back and forth, so when Mark Zuckerberg came, there was no discussion. Everything was already negotiated."

It was fascinating to think of Facebook as a giant plant being transplanted into the islands of Japan. Miki's friend had prepared the roots, and the transplant had taken. But I was perplexed. At first, Miki told me *nemawashi* was a bad word. But what her friend had accomplished was so public and so admirable. I pressed Miki for answers.

"Why is *nemawashi* a bad word if what your friend did is so great?" I asked.

Miki smiled and searched for a way to say something without being impolite. "It can be bad or good, but it generally means bad. Like you are sneaking," she said.

"Like back-channeling?" I asked. Miki shook her head, showing she was not familiar with the word. "You know, like *House of Cards* on Netflix? The President is always finding another way to move his plans forward." Miki started to nod vigorously. "So what is good about it? It sounds pretty bad," I said.

Miki shook her head again, disagreeing. "It is good in some ways, but people don't want to talk about it. It's not polite." Miki paused, then continued. "So why are you asking me about that word!?"

I was asking Miki about this esoteric Japanese gardening term because I was starting to believe the word might be essential to leading change, not only in Japan but everywhere.

We were honing in on a precise English translation of *nemawashi*, but to figure it out, I had to go deeper into the word's long history.

The Toyota Production System (TPS) and the history of lean management

To understand *nemawashi*, we have to rewind history to Japan after World War II and look at one Japanese company: Toyota.

Back then, Toyota was a small textile manufacturer that had turned itself into an automobile manufacturer. At Toyota, two men named Kiichiro Toyoda and Taiichi Ohno would spend the next forty years developing a new system of manufacturing that would first revolutionize manufacturing, management, and entrepreneurship around the world and in the United States. The system was first known as the Toyota Production System, or TPS.

At that time, Japanese manufacturing was playing catchup with the United States. Henry Ford had developed the United States' manufacturing strategy based on maximizing production by using the newest, fastest, and largest possible machinery. Toyoda and Ohno developed a new manufacturing process that focused, above all, on the reduction of waste and the harmony between processes. It became the standard for all Japanese manufacturing, and over the next forty years, it became the standard for the world.

The Ford manufacturing system could build many, many cars at an affordable price because it used huge standardized machinery and automation. Famously, Henry Ford said he would sell you a Model-T in any color you liked so long as it was black. In contrast, Toyota's new production system enabled quick, small-batch manufacturing. The new manufacturing program could flex and change to meet diverse consumer tastes. By the 1980s, manufacturers around the world were looking for ways to continue to use mass production while making it flexible enough to accommodate rapid changes and improvements. Toyota's production system went from being a Japanese curiosity to the model for the world.

The principles upon which Toyoda and Ohno built TPS came to be known by a series of names. In the 1980's TPS reached the U.S. and was first known as Just-In-Time (JIT) manufacturing. In 1990, the name changed again to "lean production" when James Womack published his seminal book *The Machine That Changed the World: The Story of Lean Production—Toyota's Secret Weapon in the Global Car Wars That Is Now Revolutionizing World Industry*. With Womack's book, lean production began revolutionizing manufacturing.

In 2004 an American named Jeffrey K. Liker translated lean production into lean management. In his book, *The Toyota Way*, Liker went back to the original work of Toyoda and Ohno and pulled out fourteen original principles. Liker explains how Toyota based both its manufacturing system and its entire corporate culture on these fourteen principles. Liker showed that lean was not only for manufacturing; it was also for management. Business leaders soon started applying these principles to business processes outside production, such as services, consulting, and soon software.

When Eric Ries wrote *The Lean Startup*, he adapted some of Liker's fourteen principles for the process of building tech startups. Ries applied what he learned from lean startup back to corporate innovation in *The Startup Way*, the title an homage to Liker's 2004 book.

Lean production and lean startup picked and chose between all the parts of the Toyota Production System. None of them included all fourteen principles. The primary focus was on the big three: *kaizen* (continuous improvement or iteration), *kanban* (a way of organizing and publicizing tasks into "sprints"), and *kaikaku* (making a radical change" or "to pivot").

Iteration, sprints, and pivots have entered the daily lexicon of tech and tech-adjacent companies. But while these three terms received almost all the attention of American business leaders, there were also eleven others: *hansei*, for example, translates to "self-reflection"; *yokoten* means "horizontal deployment." These two and nine others get far less airtime than the big three. But least among these principles might be principle thirteen, *nemawashi*. Liker defines *nemawashi* like this:

> *Nemawashi*—Principle 13. Make decisions slowly by consensus, thoroughly considering all options; implement rapidly.

Could we have found a new way to describe the foundation of our change model?

A shining example of nemawashi: the Lexus

An original example *nemawashi* was the development of the Lexus engine.

Ichiro Suzuki, a middle manager in Toyota, had an idea. He suggested that Toyota launch a luxury car with an engine that would exceed the speed, noise-level, and fuel efficiency of the likes of Mercedes and BMW.

When Suzuki suggested starting a new line of luxury cars, his colleagues thought he was nuts.

Audiences outside Japan have to learn one thing about Toyota. Toyota often has the reputation of being quick and innovative, light on its toes. So we might assume that Toyota is an organization open to taking creative risks and moving fast. Nothing could be further from the truth.

In Japan, people consider Toyota a conservative company that is skeptical of new technology and new processes. Toyota only moves in deliberate and risk-free steps. It is not by taking risks, but by following *nemawashi*, that this large, conservative company can move as quickly as it does and has gained the reputation globally of rapid change and innovation.

The chief engineers pushed back hard against Suzuki's new luxury car. What Suzuki was asking for was not possible. Suzuki was asking them to make an engine with tolerances that were as precise as the tools they used to make the engines. Precision tools can only make products less precise than they are, so they considered Suzuki's request physically impossible. The only way to get such high precision, they scoffed, was to build the engines by hand.

At this point, Suzuki decided to join 'Team Go For It.' He proposed that they follow the chief engineers' suggestion and build a luxury engine prototype by hand.

Suzuki had conversations with the heads of three major departments: R&D, production engineering, and the manufacturing plant. He asked each department to offer a few volunteers to form a small team of engineers to hand-build a high precision engine that would meet his stringent standards. The department heads granted Suzuki his volunteers, and the team came together and started working.

After a few months, the team succeeded in hand-building Suzuki's engine, but they did more than build an engine to specification. As this team did their work, they were thinking, observing, and inventing. They thought up new processes and procedures to increase the precision of their engines and parts. By the time they finished, Suzuki's idea of the Lexus's high-precision, luxury engine was no longer impossible.

Suzuki's work developing the Lexus and its engine was *nemawashi* at its finest. Using *nemawashi*, Suzuki made an enormous change that everyone thought was impossible inside of a sprawling and conservative company.

As I read Liker's account of Suzuki's work, I noticed eerie similarities with the process that Nikolai and I followed at Epic to launch Betelgeuse. Suzuki got an idea of a luxury automobile. He went straight to his peers. Suzuki got buy-in from three significant department heads. He took action and built a small team to make a proof-of-concept engine. It all sounded very familiar.

Building Piecemeal Consensus

What is an accurate and modern translation of *nemawashi*? And what can we glean from this word about leading change?

In *The Toyota Way*, Liker translates *nemawashi* as "consensus building":

> *Nemawashi* is the process of discussing problems and potential solutions with all of those affected, to collect their ideas and get agreement on a path forward. This consensus process, though time-consuming, helps broaden the search for solutions, and when (?) a decision is made, the stage is set for rapid implementation.

Linker's translation is excellent, but it lacks something. Consensus in most organizations is either an unreachable ideal or a four-letter word. *Nemawashi* does mean "building consensus" but not in the traditional American sense of everyone getting into a room and having a food fight.

The final product of consensus is the same everywhere, and there are two popular routes to reaching it. A team can prepare themselves to enter into a high-risk, full-contact Battle Royale of facts, feelings, and opinions. This process, if it doesn't end in consensus, often ends in rage and tears. Alternately, a team can reach agreement if everyone agrees to have a talking stick and talk timer as well as follow a laundry list of constricting rules of engagement. Such a highly regulated process, if it ever begins, often leads to hypocrisy, recriminations, and back-channeling. In either case, consensus is hard.

In contrast, *nemawashi* is a more natural and harmonious way of getting to building broad agreement, one person at a time.

What the development of the Lexus engine and Betelgeuse had in common was the building up of consensus on a piecemeal basis, one person at a time. The input of each colleague changes, refines, and improves a proposal. Each colleague becomes one strand in a web of consensus and buy-in across the organization. The web becomes the basis for an organization to adopt and implement a change very rapidly, even if it is a huge change in a conservative company.

A complete translation of *nemawashi* might be:

Nemawashi: to lead change through piecemeal consensus.

In both the case of the Lexus engine and Betelgeuse, the change depended on building up a piecemeal consensus.

First, Nikolai and I held one-on-one meetings with peers and stakeholders. Each of these meetings further refined and validated the idea and created buy-in from critical stakeholders. Once we had built this piecemeal consensus, it was safe to take action and demonstrate the idea's viability. At that point, the agreement grew until a critical mass of people all believed in the change, and they were committed to making it happen.

The missing link in lean?

Nemawashi was the runt of the litter of the fourteen principles of the Toyota Production System. It received little attention when Womack translated the Toyota Production System into lean production, and it was entirely lost by the time Ries wrote *The Lean Startup*.

Perhaps it was overlooked because it looked unremarkable. It was simply the Japanese word for something Americans already understood, such as "buy-in," "collaboration," "to make a deal." Or perhaps leaders overlooked the word because *nemawashi* looks like a cultural artifact particular to the Japanese, who, to Westerners, are obsessively polite. An American manager or CEO does not need to "prepare the roots" of the change. She only has to give the order, and it is her reports' jobs to do it.

At the time, I thought Nikolai and I had only stumbled onto a shortcut to making change and avoiding office politics. Without knowing it, Nikolai and I had been using *nemawashi* to build Betelgeuse. We had rediscovered this critical missing link. We had stumbled into how to conduct *nemawashi* within a modern American company.

After understanding *nemawashi* and translating it, I still did not understand precisely why it worked. What is the science behind bottom-up change through piecemeal consensus? To answer that, I had to look at a management theory that discovered and explained the incredible power of informal social networks at work.

7

HOW NEMAWASHI WORKS: SOCIAL NETWORKS AT WORK

The hierarchy has been the default structure of human organizations for hundreds, even thousands, of years. Its longevity is prodigious. As we saw in Part I, the hierarchy can efficiently move some information up and down an organization's ladder. Management at the top of a hierarchy can set goals and give orders to their teams. People on the front lines can report up issues and updates on their work. This efficient flow of orders going down the ladder and updates going up it makes hierarchies an optimal structure for planning all sorts of organizations.

But, as we've seen, hierarchies are not efficient when an organization wants to change or innovate. New ideas don't flow as smoothly up or down a hierarchy's official channels as orders and updates do. A hierarchy on its own has no mechanism for collecting, validating, and putting into action the ideas of every member of an organization. The structure can only efficiently take action on the ideas of the founders, board, C-suite, and high-level executives and tends to neglect the ideas of front-line managers and employees. It sacrifices flexibility and new thinking for operational efficiency.

Hierarchies stifle innovation that is coming up from the bottom.

New proposals get caught up in the gears and wheels of an efficiently running corporate machine. When those at the top order a change, those below often object, resist, or submit half-heartedly. When a change comes up from the bottom, middle managers have strong organizational incentives to block or discourage resources from going to new ideas and proposals.

The primacy of hierarchy has also diverted attention away from the power of more informal interactions at work: social networks. The study of hierarchies received far more time, attention, and research dollars. Of course, researchers knew that social networks were there. Employees obviously interacted and knew each other. They collaborated at work and socialized outside of work. However, until recently, there has been little acknowledgment that the relationships between employees constitute an extensive underground superhighway for information and authority. It is on these superhighways that a piecemeal consensus strategy for change builds, shapes, and leads change.

The discovery of social networks

The idea of social networks at work might, at first, sound trivial. A few dozen Facebook friends. A few hundred likes on Instagram per week. Joseph, Gregory, and half a dozen other folks like to hang out and watch Laker games. Do social networks at work go any further than that? As we shall see, social networks are far more expansive than a few dodgeball buddies, and a tremendous amount of information and power flow through them.

Rob Cross, a researcher at Babson College, kicked off the study of informal social networks in 1994 when he wrote the book *The Hidden Power of Social Networks: Understanding How Work Really Gets Done in Organizations*. The book is a case-by-case study of how informal social networks can be used to solve many common business issues.

Most of Cross's book strives to explain the concept of informal networks to an audience of businesspeople that have only ever learned about the hierarchy. He paints a picture of how powerful and influential social networks can be.

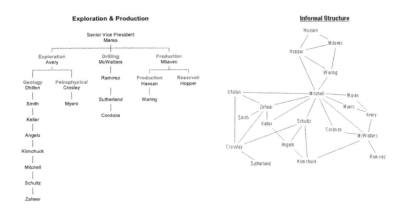

A hierarchy (left) and its social network (right) Source: The Hidden Power of Social Networks: Understanding How Work Really Gets Done in Organizations - Rob Cross

Cross raised eyebrows when he suggested that through informal social networks, an employee lower down in the hierarchy might, in many ways, wield more power than those higher up. Note, however, the above chart that contrasts the formal org chart with the informal social network shows that an employee, Mitchell, is the most connected socially, in contrast to the SVP, Mares, who, by comparison, is socially isolated.

In the second half of his book, Cross showed how organizations were unprepared to understand, improve, and leverage their social networks strategically for the value of the company. It would take decades for the world to catch up with Cross's research.

Social networks and the fountain of youth

Twenty years later, in 2007, three researchers at McKinsey studying informal networks believed they found the 'fountain of youth' for large companies.

Businesses live a life like an animal. They are born. They grow up. They grow old. And they die. But recently that started to change.

One mysterious and unexplained feature of the new economy is that some large companies continue to innovate despite their size and age. Businesses drop in productivity and innovation as they grow older and larger. But now some mega-institutions that employ hundreds of thousands of employees and have revenues in the hundreds of billions of dollars mysteriously continue to be dynamic and innovative. What is the corporate fountain of youth keeping these organizations young?

The researchers—Lowell L. Bryan, Eric Matson, and Leigh M. Weiss—used surveys and email data to research the social networks of mega-institution. They wanted to know if social networks were keeping large companies like Exxon Mobile and GE young and agile. The researchers were amazed by their findings.

The McKinsey consultant analysts could not believe "how much information and knowledge flows through [informal social networks] and how little through official hierarchical and matrix structures." Much more information goes through informal networks than through formal ones. So much so that the researchers concluded that "the formal structures of companies, as manifested in their organizational charts, don't explain how most of their real day-to-day work gets done." Looking only at the formal structure of a company's management organization was insufficient.

Thriving informal social networks, they concluded, might be the factor keeping mega-institutions young. The McKinsey researchers found evidence that leveraging informal social networks might "help to explain why some intangible-rich companies, such as ExxonMobil and GE, have increased in scale and scope and boast superior performance." There is something about informal social networks that is keeping these mega-organizations young, flexible, agile, and changeable, instead of pushing up daisies.

Two systems side by side

In Part I, we had to choose between hierarchy and holocracy. We could either have the efficiency and order of a hierarchy or the freedom and chaos of a holocracy. But not both.

Cross's and McKinsey's research into informal social networks suggests that maybe we don't have to choose. Hierarchy and informal networks have always coexisted, and over the same history of the hierarchy, there was a corresponding history of informal social networks.

Not only can these two systems live alongside each other and operate on their own sets of rules, they also depend and improve on each other. Informal social networks need the formal structures of authority and escalation to get anything done. And the traditional hierarchy needs robust social networks to strengthen itself and adapt to a changing environment.

Each person is a potential node in multiple, rapidly growing, shrinking, and shifting networks. Each network is made up of the people that are aware of and are supporting or developing one new change, process, or product. The most innovative employees are nexuses of many networks and are rapidly spawning new meshes, reaching first to their peers, and finally up to managers and high-powered individuals.

If we reach for a mechanical analogy, we might say informal social networks are like the oil to an organization's engine. They make them fluid, flexible, and reduce friction. But oil cannot retool the engine. It can't add pistons or replace the gaskets. Informal social networks can fundamentally transform their organization. A better analogy for informal social networks comes from biology.

For many years scientists believed that DNA was the totality of a cell's genetic code. Only recently did they discover that the environment in a cell can turn on and off parts of the DNA, changing the DNA's expression. There is a complex soup of proteins and catalysts in the cell that influences DNA. They called this influential genetic machinery "Epigenetics"—Greek for "on top of genetics."

Likewise, informal social networks are *epi-hierarchical*: they live on top of the hierarchies, and they can dramatically alter their hierarchy's functioning.

If a company is a biological cell, its org chart is its DNA. Informal social networks, in that case, act like the cell's epigenetic machinery. They can change and update the DNA's expression and even alter the DNA itself. A cell's epigenetic machinery allows a cell to change and adapt to its environment, just as a company that enables and develops change leadership becomes more adaptable and innovative. The networks that live on top of the corporate ladder act on that organization, changing and updating the company's DNA.

Even more recently, scientists discovered that some of the machinery in this soup could make rapid and permanent changes to an organism's structure. This piece of machinery is called CRISPR— the acronym for the delightful phrase "Clustered Regularly Interspaced Short Palindromic Repeats." CRISPR is like cut and paste but for DNA.

What Nikolai and I discovered with Betelgeuse, what I call piecemeal consensus—or *nemawashi*—is akin to CRISPR. There is a difference between the social networks made up of a random soup of dodgeball teammates and drinking buddies, and the kind of network that Nikolai and I were creating to support Betelgeuse. Our network was one characterized by a fundamental drive to develop a piecemeal consensus around one new idea. It is these sorts of deliberate social networks that, like CRISPR, make possible deliberate changes to the DNA of a company.

Leading change through informal social networks

The science behind informal social networks explains why the five steps to build piecemeal consensus are so useful for leading change: they're the practical application of this theory. They are a step-by-step guide to help anyone develop the networks they need—around themselves and throughout an organization—to lead change.

By going first to our peers, and then over and up, Nikolai and I were creating a powerful and influential social network around Betelgeuse. All change leaders who use these steps instantiate and spread their networks via private conversations and written recommendations. The networks of piecemeal consensus they create become the catalysts of change across their organizations.

In the following chapter, we'll look in-depth at each of the five steps of bottom-up change and discuss the various tactics, risks, and gotchas inside this novel way of leading change.

8

THE FIVE STEPS OF BOTTOM-UP CHANGE

So what does piecemeal consensus—*nemawashi*—look like in the modern organization? What if we cut out all the missteps and mistakes that Nikolai and I made? What if we learned from the great innovative leaders like Ichiro Suzuki and his project to build the Lexus engine? In each case, the process of change followed a five-step process that radiated a new social network out of a core of one or a pair of people.

The Five Steps of Bottom Up Change

Step 5	Take Deliberate Action
Step 4	Go Over and Up
Step 3	Write A Summary
Step 2	Start with Peers
Step 1	Brainstorm

The process of change begins with the change leaders coming up with a new idea. Next, they go to our organizational peers for feed-back and to build buy-in. They incorporate the feedback they get into a written summary of the change. Then they go over and up to get more feedback and buy-in and to develop the idea and proposal further. Finally, if the idea makes it through all those steps, you can start taking action. If taking action goes well, the idea is ready to link back up with the formal managerial structures of a business. The final step is scaling up the idea to mass adoption either internally or with customers.

Step 1: Brainstorm

Getting new ideas is tough. How do some people do it over and over again? Sitting and trying to come up with something original can feel like crossing your fingers and trying to win the lottery. However, there are a few tactics that make getting an idea easier. It is even possible to start leading change with no idea at all.

A great book on how to generate great ideas is *Where Good Ideas Come From* by Steven Johnson. Johnson studied the history of great ideas in philosophy, literature, science, business, and technology and concluded that great ideas begin with half-formed, half-baked ideas Johnson calls "hunches." When people with hunches bump into each other, their hunches combine to form the seeds of great ideas. These seeds grow into new books, theories, institutions, mathematical proofs, scientific experiments, and inventions.

The idea for Betelgeuse was the combination of two hunches: Nikolai and I both complained that knowledge management was crummy at Epic, and I discovered the open-source coding communi-ty's Q&A platforms. Those two hunches came together in our idea jam sessions in Nikolai's office.

Johnson's hunch-theory of great ideas simplifies getting great ideas. You don't have to have brilliant ideas all by yourself. All anyone has to do to have great ideas is:

1. Collect your thoughts
2. Share your proposals with others
3. Be curious about other people's ideas

Making good ideas is that simple.

How to hatch a hunch

As simple as Johnson's process is, it still doesn't answer the question: How do you develop hunches in the first place?

Nothing beats two classic strategies for developing a hunch: research and brainstorming. By going to lectures or reading books, papers, blog posts, and news and magazine articles, our brains naturally make connections into whatever topic we are researching. And, when brainstorming with others, hunches form out of the fast-paced, free-flowing conversation. But there are still other, less talked about, ways to develop ideas.

One way to develop hunches is to cultivate your inner curmudgeon. A curmudgeon takes a negative view of the world and everything in it. We might not want to become curmudgeons ourselves, but our inner curmudgeons can still help us come up with new hunches. If we ask ourselves what was the worst thing about a system, a team, or a product, the answers are often the best opportunities for improvements.

One way to illustrate this is in Seth Godin's TED talk, "This is Broken." In the talk, Godin suggests that many things around us are broken, but because we are used to them, we don't think of fixing them. Many great ideas originate from noticing what is broken, and suggesting to fix them.

Godin gave an example of a taxi stand. He saw a line of taxis in the road and a line of people on the sidewalk. Only one person was entering a taxi at a time at the front of both lines. "This is broken," Godin concludes. Both lines would disappear if everyone got into a taxi at once. Coincidentally, Seth Godin gave this TED talk the same year Lyft and Uber both released their shared rides feature—Lyft Line and Uber Pool. If we tap into our inner curmudgeon and look for what is broken around us, we'll develop more original hunches.

Godin's talk explains in part why young people and new employees are often more bent on change than older and more experienced employees. Young people and new employees are not yet used to things being broken. They can still identify them because they expect things to work.

Another way to develop hunches is to imagine starting something from scratch. Even if a project or process is years old, sit down and imagine what you would do if you were going to rebuild it starting from scratch. This sort of "what if" thinking loosens up creative ideas and gets the hunches flowing. Another version of this is to imagine you rubbed a lamp and a genie granted you one wish to change anything about a product, policy, or process. What would you change?

How to combine hunches

The second step of Johnson's process of developing ideas is to combine hunches.

The hunches that made the idea for Betelgeuse came together in Nikolai's office during our occasional idea jams. These idea jams could only happen because we could meet in and speak privately in our offices.

To develop great ideas, we have to mix it up with people in our organization.

Often commentators will use the phrase "managed chaos" to describe the climate of innovative companies. Chaotic, cross-team blending is a precursor to finding great ideas. The mixing helps people with hunches to bump into each other or spark new ideas off of each other.

If you want to find a great idea, go and chat with people, one-on-

one. Hold brainstorms and fill up whiteboards with ideas. Many will be hair-brained or impossible, but a few will hold promise.

In Part III, we'll look at how organizations as a whole can promote social mixing to support a culture of innovation and rapid change.

Starting with no idea at all

It is also possible to begin leading change without any ideas at all. All you need to do is offer to be a sounding board for others to develop and share their hunches. If others have suspicions but are not sharing them, having a place to discuss them can bring out excellent ideas.

Some questions to prompt hunch-sharing include:

- "What is your biggest challenge right now?"
- "What's one thing you would change about this process if you could?"
- "What would you do if you had to start from scratch?"
- "If you rubbed a lamp and a genie came out and said they could completely change the company, team or product, what would the genie change?"

Armed with questions like these, you can still contribute the first step of leading change by drawing out hunches and ideas from others.

Don't fall into the novice belief that getting an idea is the end of the story. Do not think "Build it and they will come," and that the world will beat a path to your door because your idea sounds good.

Once you have a list of ideas, you must prioritize which ideas you will work on first. You only have limited time and should not work on more than a few ideas at a time. It doesn't matter which plan you start to work on first, because you will see whether your idea will work or whether it needs some adjustments.

Now you've got an idea. It's time to go to work.

Step 2: Start with Peers

As we saw in Part I, a person with a new idea often starts by trying to get permission from managers or powerful gatekeepers to get it off the ground, but this strategy leads to unintended frictions and frustration. So if we shouldn't go to our managers or gatekeepers, where should we go first?

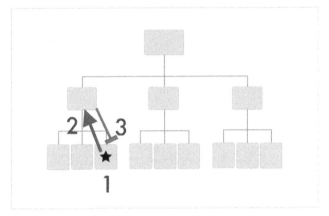

How Permission Paralysis works: 1) Get an idea 2) Escalate to manager 3) Manager brings you back to your day-to-day tasks.

Nikolai and I only started to get traction when we stopped looking for permission from gatekeepers and began getting feedback from and building a coalition of our peers. By starting with our peers and asking for feedback, we were starting a small but powerful movement within the company.

Your organizational peers are your equals. They are at your pay grade. Their level of authority is the same distance away from the C-Suite as you. If you are an entry-level salesperson, a peer would be other entry-level engineers, consultants, mechanics, etc. If you are a mid-level manager or high up independent contributor, your peers are other mid-level managers and IC's both in and outside of your role and division.

Peers are different from managers and gatekeepers in one critical way. They are impartial. That's not to say they don't have opinions and biases. They do. But peers have no direct responsibility for you or an area you want to change. Peers are open to providing valuable input and feedback and can also provide valuable buy-in. After a proposal has solidified, peers become supporters and implementers of the new proposal.

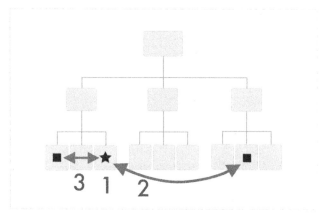

Step 2 - Start with Peers in action. First, talk to your organizational peers in and outside of your department or division.

Unlike with a direct manager, peers are on even footing. This equality makes peers better first contacts when trying to make a change. As equals, they will not be trying to reel you back into the narrow boundaries of your job role. They have a smaller vested interest in your performance than your manager, and they can't fire you. Unlike a gatekeeper, they will not assume their time is more valuable than yours. All in all, peers are easier and less risky to approach with a new idea.

Going to your peers will refine and validate your idea while building a broad coalition of buy-in across the company. If your proposal survives and adapts to the feedback of peers, and peers are interested and excited in it, it is likely to succeed. If your idea doesn't stand up to scrutiny, and no one is getting excited about it, your project might need adjustments.

Get feedback and build support

Meetings with peers can be informal. A fifteen-minute meeting—either scheduled or impromptu—works well. The meetings should be one-on-one and in private and can happen inside or outside work.

Meetings with peers are different from meetings with managers. You aren't going in worried about getting a "Yes" or a "No." You are not looking for permission. You don't need their sign off. You are trying to get honest feedback and perhaps their help and support to develop the idea further.

As with all communications, however, there are still some important things to take into account when reaching out to peers.

Don't come on too strong

No one likes the hard sell. When someone ambushes us in our office or flags us down in the hallway, we already are on our guard. If they start trying to convince us of an idea they've cooked up, we start looking for an exit from the conversation. Ambushing people with a hard sell invites people to be dismissive and critical of your idea. Instead of starting in with "I've got this idea ...," start a conversation by asking them open-ended questions about the issue or opportunity you are considering a project around.

- "What do you think of our company events?"
- "If you could improve anything about our team, what would it be?"
- "What do you think the biggest risk is to our sales team?"
- "What do you think makes our fundraising so successful?"
- "What do you think is the most costly and least impactful thing we do as a team?"

1. Listen carefully and actively

When someone says anything, repeat it back to them in your own words. Follow up with clarifying questions. If your peer is drifting towards the change you are considering, use follow up questions to move the conversation gently in that direction. If, on the other hand, your peer is going in a different direction, follow along, and see if you can learn something. Maybe they are only griping, or you might have missed the mark with your idea, and there is a more significant opportunity.

2. Get their idea before sharing your own

Once your peer has shared, they will ask you, "What do you think?" Now is an excellent time to ask their permission to share an idea you've been having. You might say: "I'm not sure, but I've talked to a few people about an idea I heard. Can I share it with you and get your feedback?" Asking someone their permission to tell them an idea opens them up. The idea stops being strictly your idea. It is something you are willing to share with others.

3. Include the weaknesses as well as the strengths of a new idea

Adding both the strengths and weaknesses of an idea achieves two goals. First, admitting outright that an idea is not perfect reduces the natural temptation to try and poke holes in a hard sell. Second, pointing out the flaws in a plan signals to your peer that you are ready for them to give honest and constructive feedback. Don't undersell an idea's potential, but do include the idea's current shortcomings and risks.

Be prepared for peers to be critical. The peers Nikolai and I first reached out to give us strong criticism. They did not go along with our original idea. They gave us critical feedback about how the project should work. Jeff changed the open-source project I at first picked out. Eric and his colleagues told us to improve the design and demanded additional features. Everyone agreed that the name "Betelgeuse" was weird.

By listening to their feedback and responding to it, Nikolai and I were able to write a stronger proposal. With a stronger proposal, we were able to build up a coalition of supporters that would later become the basis of the project's success.

Who's got time for that?

But who has time for all these one-on-one meetings? Won't building up consensus one conversation at a time take too long? Wouldn't it be more time-efficient to have a big meeting with a convincing presentation?

This brings us to **Presentation Bias**—the irrational feeling that there needs to be a presentation for something to be real and important. Do we need presentations? Do long slide decks and sweaty palms make an organization work better? The answer is no. Despite how universal they are in organizations, presentations are quite costly and risky. In Part III, we'll see why Jeff Bezos of Amazon banned presentations, but for now, let's look at how a series of one-on-one meetings can be more time-efficient than giving a big presentation.

When thirty people attend a one-hour meeting that takes thirty total work hours, one hour for each person in the meeting. Now contrast that with someone conducting, on average, one ten minute, one-on-one conversations with each of the thirty people. That would only take 300 minutes per person, so a total of 600 minutes—or ten hours—of total work time. That is one-third the time it took to have a one-hour meeting on the topic with the same people.

Even if the leader has to double back and have more one-on-ones with some teammates, they can have three ten-minute meetings with every single person on the team before they would be less time-efficient than having a big presentation.

So one-on-one meetings take less time, but they also are more effective. Unlike presentations, one-on-one conversations refine ideas, build buy-in, and socialize their adoption all at once.

Having to present a new idea to a group feels like running the gauntlet on a tightrope wire. The presenter does their best to inform and convince everyone in the room of their idea. But audiences are naturally critical and skeptical of new ideas at first, and it is almost impossible for a presenter to address everyone's concerns during one presentation or one meeting.

If you polled the room after a presentation, not everyone would be in agreement. Not everyone probably even fully understood the presented proposal. So there will still be significant effort after a presentation to build buy-in to any idea, but not so with one-on-one conversations.

Decision-making meetings can only go on for so long, and the clock typically runs out before a group can reach consensus. Then, one of two things occur. Either, like a game of hot potato, the last thing that was talked about becomes the decision or the **HiPPO— the highest-paid person in the office**—will decide. The HiPPO might apologize that not everyone agrees but insists, for the sake of time, that the team needs to move on. They might lament that the team is so busy it doesn't have enough time to get to consensus.

By using a one-on-one approach with your peers, teams can find the time to reach consensus before the decision-making meeting begins.

Step 3: Write a Summary

When you start having conversations with peers, it is essential to capture and distill all the information you are gathering into a brief document.

Nikolai and I could have done a better job of this when we developed Betelgeuse. In retrospect, not writing things down slowed us down. We were learning, but because we didn't capture the details, we forgot things, and we had to repeat ourselves to new stakeholders. By documenting what we were learning and the decisions we were making, we would have always had an up-to-date executive summary. We could have explained the project to anyone we wanted. When the project did reach its tipping point and began scaling across the organization, if we had had such a document, the handoff to another team would have been smoother.

The exact structure of what you write down doesn't matter, but make sure it is not biased, to the point, and easy to read. Various templates exist, and all of them have the same main points. At Epic, we used a format adopted by doctors to document and make medical decisions known as SBAR, which stands for Situation, Background, Assessment, Recommendation. Although SBAR originated in medicine, it proves to be an excellent way for anyone to track the development of a change.

Doctors use SBARs every day to make complex, life-and-death medical decisions, so the format works well for organizational decision-making, even if the issues are complex and high-stakes. I've used SBARs to make significant changes to in-production software products, updating multi-million-dollar budgets, adjusting the makeup of billion-dollar health systems' legal medical records, and more.

Here is a sample SBAR for the fictional proposal to buy standing desks for an office. Although purchasing standing desks might be trivial, it's often these sorts of environmental adjustments that cause significant stress and unhappiness in the workplace: best to take a few extra minutes and jot down the issue and its solution.

∼

Situation

Should the company purchase standing desks for employees who want them?

. . .

Background

Recent publications concerning the health risks around a sedentary lifestyle have popularized standing while working. Some people have requested standing desks to improve their health and ergonomics.

Assessment

Our company already provides a $200 ergonomic fund for any employee.

Electric standing desks range from $200 to $2,000. A survey found standing desk advocates would be happy with the $800 standing desk price range. Working electric standing desks have a resale value.

For $180, there is a foldable desk addition that turns any desk into a standing desk.

People who want to stand would also like a $40 stress mat to stand on.

Better health and ergonomics can decrease the health costs of workers leading to lower insurance premiums paid for by the company.

Recommendation

We recommend increasing the ergonomic fund to $300 and buying a standing desk addition and stress mat ($220 total) for anyone who would like to stand while working out of their increased ergonomic fund—leaving them with $80 of additional ergonomic money left.

The recommendation is not a history of every permutation the idea went through. It is an up-to-date summary of an idea. It is not necessary to tell the story of how you started with the intention of changing the way your organization does sales calls, but ended up improving lead generation. It is more important to explain the situation and solution you are trying to fix or improve.

The **Situation** section should be very concise—one or two sentences that describe the situation, issue, problem, or opportunity that you are facing.

The **Background** section is one or two brief paragraphs about how the issue or opportunity got to where it is now and any relevant details from the past.

The **Assessment** section includes a summary of the relevant data and metrics that ought to inform the change.

The **Recommendation** section (which can often be the longest) consists of the various options for action, each with its pros and cons. If possible, highlight one of the options as recommended. Once you decide on one recommendation, mark it as the final choice.

It is best if you can keep these documents no longer than two pages: one page printed front and back.

Be intentional about the audience with whom you share the recommendation. At first, the document ought to be private—only a record of your notes. As your patchwork of colleagues grows, share the recommendation among the coalition of supporters for the change. The idea will still be incomplete and could change, so people need context when they first hear about the concept. Once the new plan is growing across an organization, you can broaden the document's audience.

A written recommendation is critical for organizing feedback and new information as you refine an idea and build a coalition of buy-in around it. But a significant value of a written recommendation will come long after an organization implements the proposal.

Like clockwork, about three months after an idea goes into action (and again, after six months), someone will utter the following words: "Why are we doing this anyway?" Most of the time, this person will have genuinely lost the thread of what's going on. But they might have just realized that the change pinches their toes, and they are getting cold feet. Or the forgetful person has been against the move from the beginning, and is now using a particularly passive aggressive way to strike at it. Whatever their motivations, you need protection against this destructive question.

Without a written recommendation, this simple question can act like a gust of wind that blows over a house of cards. However, if you wrote everything down, this question becomes no more than a speed bump. If someone cannot remember why the team adopted the proposal in the first place, they can re-read the document.

Once you have drafted and iterated on a change, the next step is to take some direct action. To understand this next step better, we can look at the experience of a design team lead at a major company in Silicon Valley.

Step 4: Go Over and Up

Change requires buy-in from everyone, but especially the buy-in of people higher up the organizational ladder. Once you've spoken to your peers, begin connecting with people with more experience and authority. Still, avoid going directly to your manager. Even if an idea is stronger and has a small coalition, the same dynamics of Part I are still at play. It is a manager's job to focus us back on our day-to-day work.

Nikolai's boss was the CTO of the company, and my boss was one of the top consultants at the company. But we didn't go to either of them. Either one would have shrugged us off, or thrown us into the encouragement death spiral. Instead, Nikolai first got a consulting lead named Eric onboard, and we both reached out to staff, consulting, and engineering leaders.

Instead of going directly up the management hierarchy, go to people who are over and up from your role. If you are in sales, talk to an operations manager or report. If you are in operations, speak to a manager or a report in implementation or engineering. These higher-ups will have experience and knowledge to draw on to help your project. And since you do not report to them, they will be more open to offering some of their time and more open-minded about your idea. They are not incentivized to draw you back into your day-to-day work or keep you in your lane.

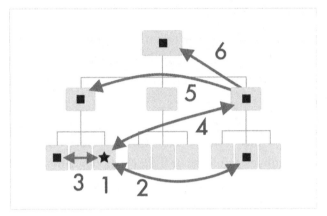

Step 4 - Go Over and Up in action. Once you've developed a recommendation, discuss the proposal with someone who is more experienced but not your direct manager or your manager's manager.

By crisscrossing your organization, you find people who have a different experience than you and more authority. The right people will accelerate the development of an idea. They will add excellent perspectives to yours, add their sway to your coalition, and connect you with more great people. If possible, go to people who already have a reputation for being interested in new ideas and change.

The conversation is the same as with a peer, except being even more respectful of the person's time. Come with open-ended questions and be appreciative of their input. Communicate in a way that includes them in the project and shows that you value their contributions.

Beware, however, that even a well-meaning higher-up might still try to discourage you or send you into an encouragement death spiral. Use what constructive feedback they give you, but you don't have to do everything they say—another bonus of them not being your manager.

Going over and down

When you are the boss, you can't go much higher, so you'll want to go over and down. When you go chat with people with less responsibility, authority, and experience than you, the interaction changes a little bit.

Going to a direct report can cause as many problems as going to a direct manager. Since you are their boss, a direct report might give you skewed feedback to please or flatter you. They may think that by you asking for their opinion, you are assigning them to work on your project. There is less confusion and better information if you speak to the reports of other managers on other teams.

Talking to people lower down the hierarchy can be very valuable. They can make influential members of a coalition and provide excellent insight and feedback. They will often be able to tell you what some unexpected consequences of a change may be. Knowing the downstream effects of a change is critical to building buy-in and designing a successful implementation plan. Be careful, though. These contacts might be more talkative about an exciting new idea. Only include them once you want more publicity and awareness.

I'll discuss going over and down in more depth in Chapter Ten, which looks at how CEOs and executives can lead change through piecemeal consensus.

Risks and gotchas

Going to over and up is a better strategy than going directly to your manager with a new idea, but there are still risks and gotchas. Here are some of the common issues with going over and up and some strategies you can employ to solve them.

Build a broad coalition

One risk is building a narrow coalition in which all the members are only within one role or division. If the team surrounding an idea is all engineers or all from the marketing division, it is in a weaker position to enact company-wide change. Your proposal will be missing critical perspectives from those other roles and divisions. And your idea cannot sweep through the company if the coalition that supports lives only in one area. Instead, build a broad coalition, not a narrow one.

Choose the right people

Avoid reaching out to personalities that could cause chaos for your project. People who gossip put a plan at risk by leaking knowledge too quickly to too many people. They also often misrepresent or embellish an idea.

Be wary of going to people who are very ambitious and willing to play cut-throat office politics. They can be a risky bet to include in a new project. Even if they might have valuable insights or powerful sway in the company, the risks of adding them might outweigh the benefits. Their behavior will be hard to predict since you won't know how your proposal fits into their plans. Only include them if you are confident that your incentives are aligned.

Reach out to people who are reliable and have integrity and with whom you share (or can quickly build) mutual respect. Go with your gut. If you get a queasy feeling when you think about working with someone, cross them off your list for now.

Don't grow the coalition too quickly

As you go over and up, be careful not to let the circle of people you reach out to grow too fast. You will change and modify your idea each time you have another conversation. If information moves too quickly and gets into the wrong room, someone might try to squash your recommendation while it is still growing.

Sometimes it is hard to direct the flow of information, but it is possible. For example, imagine someone says, "I'll ask Mariana about this," and you don't want them to talk to Marianna yet. In this case, you can communicate that, while you want to be open about the project, the idea is still fluid and not fully developed. You can say something like, "This idea isn't ready for prime time, yet. Let's get the proposal written and dialed in better before we talk to Marianna." If you are honest and don't come off too confident, you can trust that people acting in good faith will respect your request and be discrete.

Anticipate the angry manager

One considerable risk is giving managers above you the impression that you are going over their heads. One angry manager can hurt a new project. If someone feels like you are going over their head or deliberately leaving someone out of the loop, they might try to put the kibosh on your entire project. So do not intentionally try to go above anyone's head, and avoid being perceived like you are.

Keep some perspective

Being overexcited about an idea or exaggerating the idea's importance can draw criticism from peers and higher-ups. Sometimes an idea can feel like the most exciting or essential thing you are working on, but it is critical to communicate about its importance in a balanced way. Keep in mind that any new idea is necessarily going to involve a small and informal team, and the whole concept is at an experimental stage. No new idea is something worth bragging about, yet.

If a project starts moving quickly and gaining broad support, that is the crucial time to go to your manager or supervisor. They ought to hear about your involvement and leadership from you first. Otherwise, you might be going over their heads.

When you do talk to your direct manager about a project, treat them as another potential supporter. Use your listening skills to show you value their feedback, and don't disagree with them even if they believe that the project is destined to fail or is a waste of the company's or your time. Take all their feedback and thank them for it. It is not your responsibility to defend the project against all nay-sayers.

Your manager could still stand in your way, and it is your job to reduce that risk. Listening to a manager and incorporating their feedback increases the likelihood that they will support or not object to your proposal. They might even suggest you dedicate some of your formal work time to it. If you get cagey, apologetic, defensive, or arrogant, you can bet your butt they will make your life more difficult.

As the idea develops, and the coalition grows, the next important step is to keep track of your recommendation in your summary document. This document will come in handy again and again as the idea develops and someday when your team formally adopts the change.

Step 5: Take Deliberate Action

Susmita manages a large design team that was struggling with change. At a recent offsite meeting, her research team was up in arms. They felt frustrated and apathetic. They wanted to make some vital changes but couldn't. They encapsulated all this frustration and pain into one phrase they repeated like a mantra: "We are not empowered."

Susmita wanted nothing else than her research team to be empowered. But the team was suggesting that she was the one making them feel disempowered. But that was not her intention at all. Susmita was not a despotic manager or a bottleneck to change. Like many managers, she wanted her teams to be autonomous and empowered. As a manager, she wanted to know what people were doing, but she rarely stood in anyone's way. Nevertheless, her whole research team was coming to her now complaining of feeling disempowered for months.

Susmita decided to dig in. What was going on? How were they disempowered?

The team felt like they had recommendations to make to other groups, and they wanted to make seismic changes to their team. They had discussed these changes, and all agreed. But they maintained they were not empowered to make change.

"What would have to happen to make you feel empowered?" Susmita probed. The research team couldn't say.

After a whole morning discussing the ins and outs of empowerment, Susmita made a suggestion.

"How about you just go for it?" she said.

There were a few nods from around the table, and the conversation continued another twenty minutes without addressing Susmita's suggestion. Everyone broke for lunch. It took until after lunch for Susmita's advice to sink in.

The research team came back after lunch with a big announcement: "From now on, we are Team Go For It." There was a literal round of applause.

Susmita's research team already had power, but their permission paralysis had deprived them of it. Declaring themselves Team Go For It was their moment of liberation.

How to take deliberate action

The final step of leading change is to join Team Go For It. After we've got an idea, gone to our peers, written a summary, and gone over and up, the final step is to *take deliberate action*.

Taking action is the final and critical step to making change. Once you've refined the idea for change and built a coalition around it, change can still languish if you don't take action.

Taking action can mean different things in different situations. It could mean taking the classic route of making a proof of concept, but it doesn't have to. Taking action means making your idea have some expression in the real world. That expression could be actual implementation, but it could also be an expression that demonstrates the value of the change or its breadth of support.

In the case of Betelgeuse, we could have saved months if we had joined Team Go For It right away. Instead, we spent almost four months running around asking permission from gatekeepers. Suzuki would have never been able to build the Lexus engine if he hadn't pulled together a team to build the first engine by hand.

In the case of something simple, such as the question of buying standing desks, taking action might mean buying one and expensing it. Buying one of the $180 foldable standing desk extensions is not changing the policy that everyone can have one. But once one is in the office, it will be easier to decide whether everyone ought to have the option to have one. On the other hand, if your operations team is against standing desks, they will blow a gasket if they see you went ahead and bought one. An alternative way to take action could be starting a group that goes for a walk or takes active breaks once or twice a day. Taking better care of yourself is a demonstration of the value of better ergonomics.

In the case of adopting new software, if possible, sign up for a free trial and start using the software right away. Invite some of your peers to use it and give you feedback. If it is helpful, trying it out is the best way for people to get excited about a new piece of software.

If you want to change the script for sales calls, try conducting the next sales call according to your new tactic and see if it works. If you're going to suggest the team improve the look and feel of reports, produce some reports in the new style. If you want to make a new product, make a prototype on paper or digitally using easy-to-use prototyping software.

Deliberate action means deliberating about it first. It means taking actions that are risk-free or at least considered and calculated.

There is never a reason to risk your career or break any laws or company policies. We all bear the responsibility to take action if we believe we can help our organization, our clients, and the world. Taking some small risks and bending company policies is sometimes necessary for change.

Rear Admiral Grace Hopper says to just go for it

There has been no more vocal opponent of permission paralysis or more vocal proponent of taking action than the famous computer scientist and software engineer, U.S. Navy Rear Admiral Grace Hopper.

As she gained notoriety later in life, Hopper was asked to do more and more interviews. A brief review of those interviews reveals that she could not complete a conversation without going on the record urging people to stop asking permission and join Team Go For It.

> That brings me to the most important piece of advice that I can give to all of you: if you've got a good idea, and it's a contribution, I want you to go ahead and DO IT. It is much easier to apologize than it is to get permission.
>
> GRACE HOPPER, THE FUTURE: HARDWARE,
> SOFTWARE, AND PEOPLE IN CARVER, 1983

In another interview, Hopper goes even further.

"Humans are allergic to change," she said. "They love to say, 'We've always done it this way.' I try to fight that. That's why I have a clock on my wall that runs counter-clockwise."

The permission paralysis Hopper encountered and fought throughout her career might have been limited to an organization as large and conservative as the Navy. Agile tech companies in San

Francisco can't be suffering from the same problem, can they? But permission paralysis is universal.

What causes permission paralysis? Is it learned behavior, or is it part of our biology? Maybe we are allergic to change?

Maybe we are trained to wait for permission to take action from when we are children or inside traditional forms of schooling. Perhaps permission paralysis is a rational response to our society punishing mistakes more than rewarding successes. A failure, a mistake, a thoughtless phrase, or momentary irresponsible action can become a blot on our records that is hard or impossible to erase.

Hopper is suggesting that humans might have an in-built bias against change. If we look at history, there is strong evidence for this. That would explain why permission paralysis is so pervasive and why change is a challenge everywhere, not only in organizations as big and unwieldy as the Navy.

If we are going to lead change, we need to remind ourselves to keep moving forward even if it feels a bit awkward. Maybe we all need a few clocks that go counter-clockwise.

9

REWIND: THE FIVE STEPS IN ACTION

U sing what we've learned about social networks, and how to lead change with the five steps, let's rewind and look at the three case studies we started with:

1. **Tom**—the humble assistant ad buyer at Turnstyle
2. **Molly**—the rising czar of Corporate Social Responsibility
3. **Brooke**—the ambitious automotive innovator

Tom at Turnstyle

Tom already had some great ideas for Turnstyle, so step one was already complete, but he had severe permission paralysis.

Tom blamed his closed-minded manager and micro-managing CEO for his failure. But from my perspective, Tom's manager and CEO at Turnstyle weren't doing a bad job. Managers and executives ought to keep people in their lanes. They ought to keep their reports focused on their core job tasks. It was Tom's responsibility, not management's, to move in and around the organization and be a leader of change.

Let's look at each idea Tom had in order and imagine a strategy for making each one a reality.

1. Using analytics better
2. Fixing the bias in interviews
3. Focusing on either large or medium-sized clients

Tom had to ask himself, which change should he work on first? The answer is to start with the one that looks the least risky and the easiest to pull off.

The most straightforward idea on Tom's list was fixing the biased interviews. The HR team could make a small announcement to interviewers, warning them not to talk between interviews, or they could schedule the interviews back-to-back. But even though the problem was relatively simple, Tom might have felt daunted trying to lead a change outside of his department. So let's imagine that Tom started with trying to improve things within his team. How could Tom get the advertising team to enhance its use of analytics?

Improving analytics

Tom needed feedback and buy-in from his peers. He had easy access to fellow assistant ad buyers and other entry-level people in other departments. If we imagine Tom chatting with another assistant ad buyer named Jesse, the conversation might sound something like this:

Tom: Did you see the numbers from last week's campaign?

Jesse: Yes, but careful with those. I'm not sure how accurate those are.

Tom: Jeez. I wonder if there's anything we could do to have better numbers to work with. What do you think?

Jesse: Not sure. Maybe talk to Betsy about that?

Tom: Not a bad suggestion. It's not the tool we use, that looks to be okay. It is just the setup, right? Have you ever tried to make custom reports?

Jesse: I know it's possible, but I haven't done that. I just use the templated ones.

Tom: Well, if I make a few custom reports, can I shoot them by you to get your feedback?

Jesse: Sure.

That is not an earth-shattering conversation by any means, but it does its job. Tom got some validation from Jesse that his idea is not entirely off-base. Tom also got some feedback and some buy-in. After a few more one-on-one conversations like this one, Tom wrote up what he learned in a one-page recommendation. Inside the document, Tom listed the shortcomings of the current solution and the pros and cons of other options.

Tom was ready to go over and up. He ought to avoid going to the ad buyer he supports with his idea. Go to another ad buyer instead—ideally one who has complained about weak metrics and reporting in the past. After getting some feedback and buy-in from a few more experienced people, Tom had a few options for taking action.

Option #1 - He could implement a demo of better analytics and set the old and new solutions side-by-side. Comparing and contrasting between the two would make an excellent follow-up meeting with the assistants and ad buyers he had met with at first.

Option #2 - He could volunteer to teach a lunch-and-learn on existing analytics platforms and strategies. Casting himself in the role of a teacher would establish him as someone knowledgeable on the topic of analytics. During the lunch-and-learn, Tom could have attendees brainstorm ways in which analytics could be used better at Turnstyle. A brainstorm might generate new ideas and get people excited about making a change. Afterward, Tom would have a perfect segue to conduct more private conversations.

With a little luck and perseverance, there is a good chance the change would work.

Biased interviews

The next idea Tom had was to fix biased interviews. Tom had noticed that interviewers talked to each other between interviews, and this was biasing hiring. This was not a complicated problem, but it was an HR problem outside of Tom's department. How could he tackle this one?

As with the analytics problem, the next stage was for Tom to get input and buy-in from his peers. Recruiting coordinators were Tom's peers since their role sat at about the same organizational level as assistant ad buyers. Tom could strike up some one-on-one conversations with recruiting coordinators and ask if they saw interview bias. What did they think the solution was?

His peers might already know whether the problem exists or not, and will have solutions at the ready or not. In any case, it won't hurt for Tom to ask. And, given a chance, Tom could suggest a solution: coordinators could schedule interviews back-to-back as much as possible and make a small announcement to interviewers asking them not to discuss interviews except during hiring meetings.

These are plausible and straightforward solutions. Tom could hope that they would gain traction in the minds of the recruiting coordinators. Recruiting coordinators might be able to solve the problem of biased interviews on their own, so there would be no need to go through building a large coalition of managers who are over and up from Tom's position. If, however, the recruiting coordinators are disempowered from making such a change and not comfortable going to their managers, then going over and up becomes a viable option.

Whether Tom only has to have a few conversations with some recruiting coordinators, or go over to his peers and then up to managers throughout the organization, it is feasible to think Tom could lead change even in another department.

Medium vs. large clients

The last idea Tom had for change was the most ambitious and the most challenging. Tom noticed that medium and large-sized organizations needed very different services from Turnstyle. He believed that it would be more efficient and profitable (and less crazy-making) to focus on serving one client segment well instead of splitting the company's efforts and serving both poorly.

This was a CEO-level decision. How could Tom start a change this big as an assistant ad buyer? It might have taken some time, hard work, and some luck, but I believe Tom had a pretty good chance at success if he was committed to leading the change. After getting an idea, Tom should have started by going to his peers.

Let's imagine Tom started building consensus inside the advertising team. Tom found that his fellow assistant ad buyers agreed. It was causing brand confusion and costing the company too much money to target two different types of customers.

Next, Tom went to his peers in other departments. If focusing on too many client segments was spreading the company thin, the adverse effects would be visible all over the company. Perhaps during lunch, Tom reached a few sales assistants, a few junior designers, and some junior account managers. One-by-one, Tom asked them what their biggest challenges were. Each of Tom's peers validated and added nuance to his idea. Tom has become one of the best-informed people at the company on this issue.

After getting feedback, validation, and buy-in from his peers, Tom would be ready to write a recommendation document. The document contained a brief expression of the problem and proposed some possible solutions.

Armed with validation from peers and his recommendation document, Tom could go over and up and start conversations with managers and executives above him. If Tom's idea were going to work, managers from other departments would continue to validate and improve Tom's recommendation.

Once Tom had built a hard core of consensus that included peers and some managers, he would be ready to take action. But which action should Tom take?

Let's imagine that Tom discovered in his research that Turnstyle was spreading itself thin because the sales team went after too broad a set of leads. If Tom could bring focus to the sales team's efforts, the problem would solve itself even without involving higher-up executives.

Tom decided to connect with a few partners on the account management team and to use what they told him. He developed more sophisticated and targeted customer avatars. He went back to his account team contacts for validation and showed the avatars to his coalition. Eventually, Tom's recommendation and client avatars ended up on the desks of sales executives and the C-suite.

If Tom and his small team did their homework and succeeded in making a lucid recommendation and insightful new client avatars, they could help focus the company towards one client segment.

Managing risks and information

If Tom takes on helping the HR team conduct better interviews or the sales team develop better customer personas, doesn't he risk over-stepping his role of assistant ad buyer and getting in trouble with his manager?

There are risks to leading change in an organization, but these risks are manageable through proper prioritization and control of the flow of information.

Tom should avoid at all costs going over his manager's head or attempting to change his job description. As long as he continues to complete the work that is assigned to him by his manager, he can stay out of direct trouble. But what if Tom's manager catches him? What if they ask him about one of his other projects directly?

It is important to remember that Tom isn't doing anything wrong. Leading change is not, in itself, dangerous, illegal, or immoral. He isn't stealing from the company or lying to customers. Tom is involved in a few small, experimental projects that take up less than a few hours per week of his time. Managers might be curious, but they should not be outraged. A good manager ought to be delighted.

Moreover, the benefits of leading change are worth the risk. While at Turnstyle, Tom will develop the reputation of a leader who is ready for more responsibilities. And after his time at Turnstyle, the changes he led will make eye-grabbing bullet points on his resume.

Besides the benefits to Tom's career, the changes he might lead would be very valuable for Turnstyle. Tom's leadership would have saved his company the $300,000 they spent on consultants on top of the incalculable amount of money saved in improved analytics, hiring, and client segmentation.

Molly the CSR czar

Like Tom, Molly already had a great idea for change. She wanted to create a CSR policy for her company, but she, too, was stuck in permission paralysis. Molly was spending an enormous amount of time and energy, asking permission from her manager and tackling to-dos on the encouragement death spiral.

As we've learned, it is natural to believe that going to one's manager with new ideas is the right strategy. Eventually, every successful new plan will need to be incorporated into an organization by management. But new ideas rarely flow up through the management hierarchy; instead, they flow around and through the organization, and finally percolate up to leadership.

Molly initially felt inspired to build a CSR policy, but trying to convince her manager to give her permission was making her anxious and frustrated. Building piecemeal consensus around a change removes frustration and anxiety because it puts the change leader in the driver's seat.

How could Molly have followed a bottom-up and piecemeal strategy of leading change?

Molly's first step would be to have some brief, one-on-one conversations with her peers. Remember, Molly had an airtight pitch that was not getting feedback or building buy-in. She was acting like everyone was against her, and she had to defend her idea from all attackers. To be a successful leader of change, she would have to dispense with the ideas of winning and losing heroes and foes, and instead use a strategy that works.

Starting with open-ended questions

Molly needed to learn how to float an idea past a colleague, not force it on them. She needed to develop an attitude and an approach that yielded feedback and buy-in.

The first step would be for Molly to start conversations with peers with open-ended questions. For example, "How do you think the company could be more environmentally friendly?" or "What are some environmental or green initiatives our company already does?"

Molly has to be extra careful because her idea has a righteous edge to it. She runs a significant risk of her colleagues feeling like Molly is forcing change on them, instead of feeling like they are part of the positive change. No one likes to feel like they are being guilted into something. Molly must build an iron-clad consensus before acting. She must collect and include her colleagues' perspectives in her final idea.

Imagine Molly has a peer named Katherine, who might be open to the idea of CSR. An initial conversation with Katherine might go something like this:

Molly: Hi Katherine.

Katherine: Hi Molly, what's up?

Molly: I was just reading the news.

Katherine: What did you read?

Molly: It is quite a bummer on most days. Especially news about the environment.

Katherine: Yeah, I became vegetarian a few months ago to try to do my part.

Molly: Wow, that's really great. I wonder what else we could do around here to help?

Katherine: I don't think folks would go for it. The company just wants to make money.

Molly: I feel the same way sometimes. But maybe there are ways we could be more environmentally friendly and save the company money, or improve the brand, or even get positive press.

Katherine: Like what?

Molly: Have you ever heard of CSR, Corporate Social Responsibility?

Katherine: I've heard the term.

Molly: It's not a silver bullet or anything, but it seems to be a way that companies can go a little greener. A few people from each team meet every month and consider what could be done to help—maybe save some money to or get some good press. What do you think?

Katherine: I like the idea, but it will be hard to get the logistics team to join. They won't want to hurt their budgets switching to greener solutions, and finance is run by John, who I'm pretty sure thinks the climate crisis is a hoax.

Molly: Great points. Sounds like, to start with, the CSR policy should only suggest changes that would make or save the company money. That should give John nothing to complain about. I'm going to talk to a few more people about it and write up a little proposal. Can I send it to you for feedback after I've drafted it up?

Katherine: Sure, thanks.

. . .

This conversation takes less than five minutes and from Katherine's perspective feels warm, inviting, and friendly. Molly isn't selling anything; she's seeking Katherine's perspective and help. Molly gleans some vital information about John and the logistics team that will help her to craft the first version of a CSR recommendation. With these pieces of feedback, Molly is already more certain the CSR won't be dead on arrival or brushed off as wishful thinking.

After four or five conversations with peers across various divisions, and writing a brief proposal, Molly can go over and up. She might start with a middle manager in the finance team—someone who works below John—to feel out how big of a problem building consensus with that team will be. Let's imagine this person's name is Sonja.

Molly: Hi there, thanks for meeting with me.

Sonja: Of course. Come in. What can I help you with?

Molly: I was reading an article a few weeks ago about how companies were saving money by becoming more ecologically friendly, and I started to think about our company. Do we have any sort of green policies or proposals going on?

Sonja: I think a year ago or so there was a bit of a crackdown on printing paper. Some folks set all the printers to print on both sides, and we switched to recycled paper. That's all I can think of.

Molly: Oh, that's great.

Sonja: Well, it is expensive paper, even if you print on both sides.

Molly: Right. Of course. Do you know if there has ever been any sort of corporate social responsibility team?

Sonja: The company does some charitable giving, and the CEO has his issues that he does some giving around, and each fall, each employee can direct some funds to the charity of their choice.

Molly: I really like that we do that! One idea that I've read about and heard thrown around a few times is creating a corporate responsibility team that meets periodically to run social responsibility projects. From your experience, what are your thoughts on making a team like this?

Sonja: In theory, it sounds possible. It sounds a lot like our employee happiness team.

Molly: I hadn't thought of the similarities with employee happiness. Who do they report to?

Sonja: The chairperson of that committee reports to HR, I think. This team you're describing might want to connect with someone in operations, although I'm not sure.

Molly: Great thanks for the suggestions. I'm writing up a proposal for these ideas. Would you be available to look over the proposal once it is written?

Sonja: Sure, I can look at it, but I can't say if it will be approved.

Molly: That's alright. I appreciate your feedback and experience. Thank you very much. This helped a lot. Bye.

In this five-to-ten-minute conversation, Molly was giving Sonja some deference and paying respects to her experience and power. Molly was asking so many questions, and she was not pitching anything or asking permission. She did a good job warming Sonja to her project and getting constructive feedback on how to proceed.

Once Molly has updated her document with Sonja's feedback, she is ready to take some action.

Taking deliberate action

Taking action is an art, not a science. There is no formula. A change leader and their collaborators can choose from several different directions to go in. What action you take depends on the idea and the situation. What action you finally select ought to be both low risk while still demonstrating the value of the idea and the strong consensus around it.

In the case of CSR, let's imagine Molly went ahead and scheduled the CSR's first meeting, but she didn't call it that. It was only a meeting to review the proposal. Molly played it safe and invited people who would be useful members of a real CSR team. She picked from people she had already approached for one-on-one conversations, including those with a keen interest in CSR, that represent a diversity of opinions (even ones she disagrees with), and come from diverse teams. Constructing a broad and diverse group will reduce the risk of backlash from people who do not feel represented.

If this meeting to review the proposed CSR team goes well, it will feel like the first CSR team meeting. Molly's proposal becomes the CSR's *de facto* charter. In some sense, Molly has now succeeded; no permission necessary! Of course, they still have to build up some momentum to become official.

At this first meeting, the team could decide on a few low-risk, easy-to-implement CSR projects that they want to tackle. Because Molly did such a great job socializing the idea of a CSR across the company, no one will be surprised that the team now miraculously exists and is taking some small actions.

If over a few months the new CSR team manages to have a few small successes, provide a dose of inspiration to the office, and not step too firmly on anyone's toes, the team will be well on its way to success. The new CSR team could soon be asking for official things like a budget. Who knows, they might even get a budget without asking. When you build a project up like this through piecemeal consensus, it often starts to attract unexpected allies.

Through one-on-one conversations, developing buy-in, writing a document, and taking action, Molly could quickly and reliably lead the change of creating a CSR team. The whole process might require five-to-ten casual meetings, each lasting five-to-twenty minutes. Molly would spend a few hours writing and editing her document, which would double as a charter for her new group. It might only take her one month to go from idea to the first CSR team meeting. It would take another month for the program to show some small successes.

Brooke, the automotive innovator

When I met with Brooke again, she was about ready to quit her job at a major automotive manufacturer. She had been working closely with her clients—fast-paced California automotive startups—and they were hiring.

When Brooke and I started working together, she was desperately trying to reach the most senior people at her organization and show them as big a mountain of data as possible to support her idea. They would have to see the strength of the data she'd found and order the change. The strategy had been a spectacular failure.

When Brooke finally did get the chance to do a pitch to some bigwigs at her company, they treated her like she was in a high school public speaking class. After this experience, Brooke was at the brink of quitting. But Brooke is not a quitter. She was not going to give up trying to crack the code of how to lead change in her organization.

In our next meeting, Brooke told me that she wanted to champion more than one idea. She wanted to champion all of them. Brooke was trying to bring what she had learned about experimentation and innovation from startups in California to her old, traditional company. At her company, they developed a strategic plan in closed-doors executive retreats. Goals and metrics came down from the top. She wanted to bring bottom-up change to her organization.

The best way to make her company more innovative, Brooke decided, was to lead by example, pick the low-hanging fruit, and demonstrate a repeatable strategy for making change. Since we were working together, she decided to try out the piecemeal consensus strategy for leading change.

Brooke's new tactic

Brooke and Molly had a lot in common. They had permission paralysis—they believed success meant going up the ladder of authority—and they had airtight arguments and compelling data for their new ideas. They also had in common that their strategies were not working.

The problem was that they were not building coalitions inside informal social networks. Brooke and Molly were too defensive about their ideas. No one felt like they were becoming a part of the team. If Brooke and Molly were going to build consensus around their ideas, they were going to need to stop going to their managers, start going to their peers, and change their approach.

Brooke immediately took to the idea of *nemawashi*. When she first heard it described, she said it felt like a weight was falling off of her shoulders. She would no longer have to be on the defensive with her new ideas and felt right away how much more natural it would be to ask people what their challenges and hunches were instead.

Asking for help and showing vulnerability is an excellent way to open people up to new ideas, gain their trust, and learn about their hunches. If we act like we have all the answers, it prompts our colleagues to poke holes, disagree, and play devil's advocate. When someone comes into our office with an agenda as fixed as steel-reinforced concrete, it is impossible *not* to think of ways to poke holes in it. Certainty often breeds skepticism. By sharing one's questions and doubts, and not giving the impression of having all the answers, we invite others into new ideas. Our colleagues begin encouraging us, instead of poking holes. They offer suggestions. They join our team.

Brooke understood the value of being more vulnerable in many situations, but suggested that it wouldn't work for her case. Her position as a woman in a man's industry altered these dynamics. She didn't want to be perceived as a shrinking violet, or as someone who needed everything explained to her by her colleagues. So we would have to develop a different approach to her situation.

We brainstormed a few questions Brooke felt comfortable using to open up one-on-one conversations with her peers. She came up with two she planned on using right away.

1. "If you started fresh from the ground up, how would you approach X?"
2. "What is the biggest challenge that Y team is having?"

We decided to meet again in two weeks. Brooke would spend that time having some open-ended, one-on-one conversations with peers and report back her findings.

Two weeks go by

After two weeks, Brooke called me back. She was excited. Talk of quitting her job was gone. The strategy had worked. She had not changed the whole company overnight, of course, but she had made more progress in two weeks than she had made in the last year.

Brooke had found her hunch. The company was doing a poor job of working with new automotive startups. It struggled for two reasons. First, sales to these startups went through casual networking rather than the traditional channels of cold calls or an old-boy network. Second, these startups focused on electric vehicles that required new products that her company had not yet developed. If they did not move fast, another startup would emerge and engineer these parts for the expanding market of electric vehicles (EVs).

We looked at the five steps and brainstormed some options Brooke could take. Conversations with two peers had already had positive results. But both of those had been in her department where Brooke would encounter the least resistance. Next, she ought to identify peers in other departments who would be open to talking about EVs.

Brooke believed that her company could serve this new EV market. She planned to start writing a recommendation document that summarized what was at stake and begin collecting solutions. I suggested the trusty SBAR format, and we started a draft together.

Brooke wanted her idea to work, but even if it didn't work out, Brooke was happy that she was setting an example for those around her of experimentation and innovation. Remember, Brooke's bigger goal was to help her whole division, and eventually, her entire company to become more innovative. As she was already seeing positive change after only two weeks, she was intent on continuing with the new piecemeal strategy.

Brooke's promotion

A few weeks later, Brooke texted me. Big news.

Brooke told me her company was announcing a massive reorganization. The executives had decided to realign the company's focus. In practice, this meant shaking up the company's org chart. Brooke was getting a promotion. She was becoming the leader of all business development within the startup ecosystem.

Brooke admitted that her adoption of a piecemeal consensus strategy did not cause her promotion directly. Her company's reorganization had been in the works for almost a year. However, the one-on-one conversations she had had to discuss electric vehicles had solidified Brooke's position. Her managers perceived her as the person best suited to connect the company with the emerging market of electric vehicle startups.

Using a piecemeal consensus strategy had reengaged Brooke with her job. She felt like she had agency, and that change was possible. More than anything, Brooke was pleased that others could learn from her example. Someday soon, she hoped, people at her organization would be as comfortable and excited about experimenting with new ideas as she was.

10

LEADING CHANGE FROM THE TOP

S o maybe piecemeal consensus is a pretty good strategy for leading change if you work in the mailroom. But what about people in the C-suite? What about if you already have power? Do you need *nemawashi*? Should you follow the five steps?

If the founder of a company or the president of a division wants to make a change, can't they snap their fingers and order it? Should people who are in charge also lead change from the bottom up? Should they spend the time to build a piecemeal consensus?

Half a decade after launching Betelgeuse at Epic, Nikolai had gone on to found a groundbreaking healthcare technology company called Redox, and I had started as the product lead of an innovative new college in San Francisco called Make School.

To understand whether bottom-up change works for those on top, I conducted a grand experiment. I decided to use piecemeal consensus to make many rapid structural changes to Make School. My experiences there have reinforced my belief that the concept of bottom-up change works better for everyone—even people at the top.

Leading change at Make School

When I arrived, Make School was already a breakthrough in higher education in many ways. The college used Income Share Agreements (ISAs) to make a computer science education available to anyone in the U.S. The college had innovated on how to pay for education. Still, it was struggling to make a better experience than traditional college.

Despite the college's forward-thinking mission, the school itself was in chaos. Students were in open revolt, instructors and staff were losing faith, and the business itself was in the red. One student compared the school to "a dumpster fire." To me, the school was a new institution of higher education in need of rapid and transformative change.

I was hired to bring significant structural change to Make School, fast. The founders gave me the authority to make any changes I thought best. However, the instructors, staff, and founders were all invested in how the school ran. I knew that if I started giving out orders, there would be friction and backlash. I would end up fighting with people I was supposed to be leading. Moreover, if I had just told people what to do, I wouldn't have included my team's feedback. And I would have done the wrong thing or acted in the wrong way.

For all these reasons, I decided it would be too risky to lead change from the top down by authority or by influence and office politics. Instead, I drew upon my time developing Betelgeuse and chose to work from the bottom up.

The result was two years of continuous and transformative change. As a result, we tripled the number of students, doubled the staff, earned official higher education accreditation, and the organization raised over twenty million dollars on the strength and outlook of the school.

Idea #1: Restructuring meetings

Every week the school held an enormous meeting that included both founders, all of the marketing team, staff, and the whole faculty. My first idea was to disinvite the faculty from meeting and pull them into a separate, smaller weekly faculty meeting. But this would not be easy. Meetings are often as resilient as they are useless and, whatever people say about them, asking people to stop attending can make them feel as if they no longer have a voice. I had an idea for how to make it all work to everyone's benefit.

I first went to Alan, an instructor who had been at Make School the longest. I asked him what he thought of the meeting and what he would change. What did he think of sending one representative of the instructors to the product meeting and holding a separate instructor meeting?

At this point, if I had given Alan an order, it would have strained our working relationship, but going to him for his opinion and feedback deepened the trust between us.

Alan agreed that not everyone needed to attend the product meeting, and he graciously volunteered me to be the faculty representative. Alan told the other instructors that they were off the hook, and they jumped for joy. I put a separate faculty meeting on the calendar.

When you start leading a change from the top, you can't go to your peers because you might have few peers or none at all. And there may be no one above you, so you cannot go over and up. Instead, you have to build consensus with people who are below you in the hierarchy of the company. You must exercise good judgment when deciding with whom to begin to build a piecemeal consensus. Here's a graphic of what that might look like:

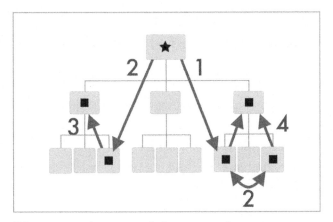

When you are at the top, instead of going over and up, you go down and over

Alan was one of my reports, but he still was an excellent first stakeholder with whom to start building piecemeal consensus. By having a casual, private conversation with Alan, the change rapidly reached consensus and buy-in.

Idea #2: Redesigning the office

The rooms and offices at Make School all lacked names, which was causing confusion and adding to the general sense of chaos in the school. Putting names to the offices might have been something I could have asked anyone's feedback, but why waste such an excellent opportunity to build trust and rapport with my team?

I pulled aside another instructor named Shannon and asked her opinion about how to add more structure and accountability to the school without negatively affecting the students' freedom. Shannon had many ambitious ideas that I filed away for later. I asked for her opinion on the idea of naming the rooms.

Shannon suggested that we name the rooms after inspiring inventors and the most important inventions of the internet. To support a balanced representation of both sexes in tech, she recommended that the inventors ought to be half men and half women.

Next, I talked to Sarah in marketing. She thought naming the rooms was a great idea, and asked if I could do the staff side meeting rooms as well.

Even though the idea was small, I wrote a brief decision document in case someone later disagreed with the change. In the proposal, I recorded the original issue, goal, and the final plan, including the suggestions from Shannon and Sarah.

I bought a laminator for $49.99, and I made signs for all the rooms and offices. The "Lovelace" office, named after Ada Lovelace, one of the first computer scientists, was across from "Tesla," named after Nikolai Tesla, the famous electrical engineer and inventor. "Hopper" named after Grace Hopper, became the new name of our board room. I dubbed our largest common area, "The Great Hall" after the Hogwarts dining room from the Harry Potter books. Finally, I put some books in a quiet room and called it "The Library."

Shannon and Sarah championed the plan of naming the offices. Shannon told the faculty, and Sarah told the staff. Students and staff started booking meeting rooms, and admissions officers began telling prospective students the story of the office rooms during tours. Everyone was excited to see our space improve and grow up.

Idea #3: Adding courses

When I started, Make School operated as a free-form school with no schedule or courses. The most prepared and self-motivated students were succeeding in this format, but the least prepared and less motivated students were not. Because of Make School's unique income share agreement model of tuition, we could not have only some students succeeding. We needed all of them to succeed. I went looking for a way to provide more accountability for students without putting the kibosh on their freedom and autonomy.

I followed my same change leadership playbook and floated the idea of starting some scheduled classes with some instructors and got some positive signals. They were willing to teach the classes. They also agreed that the courses might help support some of the less prepared and less motivated students.

Next, I went over and up and floated the idea past the founder—the one who was not my boss. He liked the freewheeling feel of Make School, and he warned me that we should not become a traditional school with schedules, lectures, and bells. At the same time, he could see that many students were struggling without structure. He trusted the instructors if they believed that having a few courses would work.

I wrote these considerations up and included an exemplar course syllabus in a brief proposal. I asked the instructors if they would each run one course. They agreed. I announced to the entire team that we would experiment with running some courses. There were nods all around, and the instructors were prepared to handle any worries brought to them afterward because I had consulted them first. Now Make School has over thirty courses, and building courses turned out to be an essential requirement for our gaining accreditation and offering a bachelor's degree.

Idea #3: Enabling students from all backgrounds

Many Make School students were struggling in ways that our instructional team and I could not fully comprehend.

At Make School, we have the privilege and the challenge of serving a student body that is diverse economically, racially, and socially. Make School makes higher education affordable to any student through income share tuition agreements. It also admits students to the program based on their passion for coding, and not based on their high school grades or SAT scores. We are also dedicated to making tech education and jobs more accessible to women. Our team faced the challenge of helping to make all the students succeed in software development when they might, at first, have felt like outsiders.

I studied what top colleges and educators were doing, or were failing to do, to improve inclusion and increase the achievement of underprivileged and underrepresented students. I found two remarkable tools I thought would benefit Make School: mentorship and one-on-one performance coaching. The research suggested that offering every student contact with a professional software engineer with a similar background to their own and assigning individual performance coaches would help all students at Make School to succeed.

Implementing such an ambitious coaching and mentoring program was the most significant change I had attempted, and it would face stiff opposition. The founders and operations team complained that the program was going to be expensive. Instructors balked at the many one-on-one coaching meetings. Who would train them to be coaches? Who would commit to the considerable work effort to find, build, and maintain a network of volunteer mentors and match them with students?

Through brief, private conversations, I was able to uncover these problems one-by-one and find solutions and compromises to each of them. Coaching might be expensive, but because of the unique incentives of the ISA tuition model, students dropping out or not getting good jobs was even more expensive. It turned out someone on our team was freelancing, in private, as a professional life coach already and was excited to train and lead our new coaching team. Our outcomes team found that, through referrals, having an industry mentor improved the chances of students getting internships. Improved placement numbers meant more and larger income share repayments, which covered the costs of growing and maintaining a network of mentors.

After about a month of building consensus one person at a time, I had created a broad consensus from the founders down to the TAs. With extensive and in-depth agreement, the team was able to put into place both programs rapidly.

The programs worked. Since we've implemented the programs, our underrepresented student drop-out rate has fallen, and student happiness, job placement rates, and salaries have risen significantly.

We have much more to do, but these two programs have been an excellent start.

Leading change as the boss

Everyone naturally doubts changes people order us to make because we haven't yet understood what the changes mean for ourselves. So top-down change always results in some level of pushback, distrust, and feet-dragging. If you order too many changes, teams will begin to experience change fatigue. However, building piecemeal consensus around changes before making them deepens the trust the team has for a boss and the engagement they have for their work and the company.

Leading change from the bottom up is not only for entry-level employees or middle managers. It is a transformative style of leadership that can get results for executives and CEOs. Anyone attempting to lead change can be more productive and successful if they build consensus one person at a time through brief, casual conversations.

Of course, I didn't get much credit. My name doesn't come up when people at Make School talk about that time. The changes felt like they were coming from everywhere at once. No one was considered the single cause of any one change. Once again, I was learning that leaders of change need to put their egos in the backseat if they are going to succeed in making something great.

PART III

BUILDING A CULTURE OF CHANGE LEADERSHIP

Culture eats strategy for breakfast.

PETER DRUCKER

11

THE HOLY GRAIL: CHANGING CULTURE

The holy grail of leading change is changing the whole culture of a company. The power to fix a broken culture is a tantalizing goal. There are so many possible changes and improvements one could make: practicing better ownership and autonomy, eliminating prejudice, improving educated risk-taking, or creating a more positive office climate. But culture can be notoriously hard to change. Some hang their heads and conclude culture is what it is. Others put up their dukes and try everything to change it.

Organizational culture is a complex and resilient part of a company. Reorgs don't have much of an effect on it. Neither does a change in leadership of those at the top. Changing hiring patterns only puts a dent in it. Even all three of these together will barely alter the edges of a culture.

All the interventions we commonly take to change culture have one thing in common: they come from the top down. But culture happens at the water cooler, in the hallway stop-and-chat, and the casual lunch conversation. Culture arises out of the context, not the content, of an organization. It would be difficult to change something inside the social networks of our organization by relying on an organization's hierarchy of information and authority. A better approach might be to make bottom-up change through an organization's social networks. That is what Uber's new CEO Dara Khosrowshahi did when he inherited the train wreck that was Uber's culture in 2017.

Changing Uber's culture from the bottom up

It must have come as a surprise to Travis Kalanick—known as "Travis"—that Uber, one of the fastest-growing and most significant tech companies of a generation, could be taken away from him because of a single blog post. But that is what happened.

On February 19th, 2017, Susan Fowler Rigetti wrote a post entitled "Reflecting On One Very, Very Strange Year at Uber." In a dry and matter-of-fact tone, she told the story of Uber's cultural hellscape that protected and promoted sexual abusers and openly promoted a "game-of-thrones political war" throughout the upper management of the company.

The blog post was a bunker-busting bombshell. Within three days, the news cycle had picked up the story. *The New York Times* wrote a piece with the tame title: "Inside Uber's Aggressive, Unrestrained Workplace Culture." Four months later, after first resisting the attacks and failing to make significant changes to Uber's culture, Travis resigned.

The new CEO, Dara Khosrowshahi, had a clear mandate to amend the toxic culture, but how could he turn around the proverbial Queen Mary of corporate culture? Only nine months after Rigetti's bombshell blog, he wrote his own post entitled "Uber's New Cultural Norms" in which he announced Uber's new culture. His approach was not precisely *nemawashi*, but he did provide an example of the effectiveness of a bottom-up approach to change in action.

"I feel strongly that culture needs to be written from the bottom up. A culture that's pushed from the top down doesn't work, because people don't believe in it. So instead of penning new values in a closed room, we asked our employees for their ideas. More than 1,200 of them sent in submissions that were voted on more than 22,000 times. We also held more than 20 focus groups with representatives from our Employee Resource Groups and our international offices."

Once Dara had established these new norms, Uber went into overdrive, making changes across the organization. The company created an "Integrity Hotline" to receive and take action faster on complaints. They doubled their investment in HR support for employees. They changed their hiring goals and achieved a new high watermark of 43% gender parity, and saw a modest 7% increase in women in leadership roles. The company's culture was changing rapidly. But were these new norms just whitewashing? Or were they working, and will they stick?

I work a few blocks from Uber HQ and have colleagues and friends who worked at Uber during and after these tumultuous times. Everyone I talked to agreed that Uber's culture had improved. None would say Uber was a leader in civility, equity, and inclusivity. Uber still had a culture of pushing limits, whether they are technological, legal, or personal. But the improvement was significant. The bottom-up changes were working.

Dara could not have secured buy-in across the company for these sorts of sweeping changes if he had handed down the new company norms after a strategic planning offsite. The process for "crowdsourcing" these norms was still quite hierarchical, and the C-Suite had the final word on what went into them. Nevertheless, by developing these norms from the bottom-up, he encouraged the buy-in from people across the organization that has succeeded in mending a broken culture.

Building a culture of change leadership

So far, this book has been about how anyone, regardless of their position or level of authority, can begin to make significant changes to their organization. In Part I, we started by looking at organizations and what are the most common strategies they employ to make change. Each plan we looked at had a hidden failing that worked against the goal of sustaining innovation and change. In Part II, we looked at a new approach for leading change called piecemeal consensus or *nemawashi*. We broke down how any individual can put this change leadership strategy into action in any organization with a simple five-step model.

In Part III, we return to looking at organizations. Like the case of bottom-up culture change at Uber, we'll look at examples of piecemeal consensus already in action, and try to learn what policies and patterns organizations can establish to cultivate a culture of change leadership.

Remember Brooke, the automotive innovator? She had the goal of changing the culture of her company. She wanted the whole company to be experimental and interested in change, instead of fearful and resistant to it. What would it be like if Brooke succeeded? If her entire company supported everyone running experiments and launching new ideas? What could they achieve if everyone knew how to lead careful and deliberate change? Is it possible to create a culture of change leadership inside an organization?

We'll look at companies, such as Amazon, Pixar, and Google, who have built and maintained a culture of innovation since their founding. These companies reveal several principles that dramatically improve and support a culture of change leadership. Those principles are:

1. Balancing the power of management
2. Social mixing during the workday
3. Building psychological safety

4. The role of innovation officers
5. Adequate privacy
6. Reconsider presentations

None of these policies is a silver bullet for building an organization with an innovative culture. Still, each one helps to lower the barriers and frictions that potential leaders of change face and increases the chances that new ideas can grow.

12

BALANCING THE POWER OF MANAGEMENT

W hen looking around for an example of an organization that supports bottom-up change, I did not have to look any further than a little internet company with a childish name: Google.

Larry Page and Sergey Brin had a hunch that the internet needed more than a search engine. The internet needed a company that was constantly innovating and advancing the organization of information. They set about constructing an organization and building an entirely new culture. This structure laid the basis for innovative products that we all know and use fifteen years later.

Many journalists have pointed out that Larry Page and Sergey Brin made Google operate more like a grad school, and less like a company. They made four-person offices like Stanford did for its grad students. Dress was casual. They strove to make their offices feel more like a college campus than a business.

Page and Brin were trying to vaccinate their company against permission paralysis by reducing the power of management and increasing the strength and independence of front-line employees. To create a culture of autonomy that Google has enjoyed for fifteen years, Page and Brin had to balance the power between management and front-line engineers and employees.

They redistributed power to people throughout the organization. People were freed to start experiments that may someday change or improve the company. The trick was how to implement policies that balance the power of management while preserving the efficiency of the organization's hierarchy.

We'll look at three of Google's most famous innovation policies—engineers electing projects, 20 percent time, and the way Google promotes managers. In each case, we'll see how the system enhanced innovation by balancing the power and influence of the management hierarchy and elevating the authority, autonomy, and influence of front-line engineers and employees.

By their own lights and designs, Page and Brin helped to free the genius, not only of executives and management at Google, but of everyone.

Persuading engineers and 20 percent time

Two of Page and Brin's early innovations were utterly unheard of in the rank and file of pre-internet technology companies.

Page and Brin forbade Google's managers from ordering engineers to work on a project. Engineers could pick which projects they wanted to work on as they wished. Empowering engineers meant engineers with great ideas could pull together teams without needing permission from management. Moreover, managers would have to sell their ideas to attract and keep engineers on their teams.

Like Valve's holocracy, Google was betting that the best people to judge fresh new internet products were the software engineers themselves. But unlike Valve, Google still had a functioning hierarchy, so they didn't have to hold lengthy meetings to vote on everything from titles to salaries.

But how did these Googlers have time to sit around, develop new products, and pitch each other to join a new team? That brings us to Google's famous 20 percent time policy.

The policy said that Googlers are free to use twenty percent of their time—roughly one day per week—on whatever they "considered to be most valuable for Google."

Critics have claimed that 20 percent time was not all it was cracked up to be. The most famous criticism came from the pen of Marissa Mayer, ex-Googler turned CEO of Yahoo: "It's really 120 percent time," Mayer said, revealing that Googlers don't literally have twenty percent of their time carved out and given to them on a silver platter. They still have to do one hundred percent of their regular work, but they were free to do more on top.

Despite Mayer's revealing criticism, in practice, 20 percent time still made a significant difference to Google employees. 20 percent time meant that Larry Page and Sergey Brin gave every employee permission to work on more than what their manager told them. And the founders forbade managers from packing their report's lives so full that there was no room for anything else.

Laszlo Bock, another famous Googler, explained how it works in his book *Work Rules!* For Bock, "the idea of 20 percent time is more important than the reality of it.... It operates somewhat outside the lines of formal management oversight, and always will because the most talented and creative people can't be forced to work." 20 percent time protected people's pet projects and the small or large changes they were leading or supporting.

Promoting managers and Project Oxygen

Another policy Google adopted to balance the power of management came after they discovered that it was promoting the wrong engineers into management. They called the research team Project Oxygen.

Google's people team decided to research why employees were leaving the company. They found a familiar pattern. The number one reason people cited when they quit was their manager: as the old

HR adage goes, "People leave people." But Google wanted to know why people were leaving their managers and how they could fix things so that they wouldn't. Focusing on engineers, Project Oxygen looked at how Google promoted people into engineering management.

The team discovered that, like many companies, Google was in the habit of promoting the best front-line engineers to become engineering managers. But the team also found out that the best-rated managers were not necessarily the best engineers.

The two jobs require separate skillsets, and one person might not be the best at both. Being a manager requires strong interpersonal skills, such as listening, empathy, and communication. Being an excellent engineer is a different skill set based on deep solo work and crystal-clear analytical reasoning. Making promotion to management dependent on competence in a different skill set was a mistake.

After making this discovery, the Project Oxygen team rewrote the rubric for what made a good manager at Google. Their research showed that it was still valuable for engineering managers to be competent engineers, but they didn't have to be the absolute best. They recommended new assessments for front-line engineers based on the skills they found a manager ought to have.

Case Study: Gmail

To see Google's culture in action, consider the story of the invention of Gmail.

Paul Bucheit had wanted to build something using email since 1996. In 2001 someone in Google nudged him to go for it and create whatever he wanted. The first thing Paul built was extremely simple: he took Google's search algorithm and pointed it at his inbox. Now he could search his email inbox with the same power and precision as Google provided for websites. Bucheit ran the initial prototype of Gmail on a computer under his desk.

Bucheit was not the only person inside Google tinkering with search, email, and other odds and ends of the new internet world. Still, it was his "email search" that became Gmail through a series of exemplary bottom-up steps of change leadership.

Google was at an inflection point and was going through hyper-growth. The goal of management was to develop new internet products based in and around its proven Google search product. To do that, they cultivated a climate of chaotic innovation. In practice, that meant they hired a bunch of smart people and let them do whatever they wanted.

Bucheit first went to his peers. He showed his three officemates his new email search engine. They liked it. They wanted to search their email, too, using Bucheit's new tool.

Once his office mates tried it, word got around that Bucheit was on to something. This sparked a debate. Remember, Google wasn't like Yahoo or Lycos that were becoming "portals" to do almost everything on the internet. Google was a search company, and providing email accounts wasn't strictly search. Many Googlers were hell-bent on Gmail never seeing the light of day.

In hindsight, it is easy to pretend that Gmail was always a sure bet, but Bucheit tells another story. "A lot of people thought it was a very bad idea, from both a product and a strategic standpoint," he told *Time* magazine. "The concern was this didn't have anything to do with web search. Some were also concerned that this would cause other companies such as Microsoft to kill us." The debate went on for three years, practically eons in the world of technology.

Executives and founders did not halo in to decide that Gmail would launch. Instead, Gmail percolated and developed, conversation by conversation for three long years. The product matured slowly, and those who saw Gmail as a viable part of the Google product suite continued to make their case in small meetings, in four-person offices, and around water coolers.

Gmail remained a complete and utter secret from the outside world. The day before Gmail's announcement, someone leaked that a Google email was around the corner. Google released Gmail on April

1st, April Fool's Day. Most commentators thought it was a joke. It took until the third or fourth of April until people realized that Gmail was here to stay.

In the next chapter, we'll look at another policy Google adopted that was critical to promoting bottom-up change: they gave everyone a free lunch.

13

MAKE TIME AND SPACE FOR SOCIAL MIXING

In 1985 the board of Apple sacked Steve Jobs as CEO. He was thirty years old and had spent the last nine years of his life building a visionary computer company. Eleven years later, in 1996, he would become the CEO of Apple again, turn the flagging company around, and lead it to become the largest company in the world. During his hiatus outside of Apple, Jobs worked with a few companies, including a small, unknown startup animation studio called Pixar.

Pixar has been and continues to be one of the most innovative companies in the world. It invented and pioneered new animation technology. Simultaneously and under the same roof, they write and produce stories that are new, moving, and overwhelmingly popular. Pixar's successes have been so colossal and so consistent that they have moved the goalposts for the entire industry of film, especially lucrative children's movies. Disney, who invented feature-length animated children's films, had to sprint and spend billions to catch up.

Pixar is an excellent case study in how to make a culture that enables change leadership, and Steve Jobs can claim some credit for developing this innovation powerhouse.

Steve Jobs was famous for micromanaging the hell out of the companies he ran, sometimes with good reason and often with excellent results. He famously micromanaged every element of the Apple II, the Macintosh, the iPod, and the iPhone from soup to nuts. Each one of these products was a world-transforming success, in large part thanks to this one man's exacting and critical eye. Pixar was no exception.

A big atrium with a single bathroom

Jobs was not the inspiration for Buzz Lightyear in *Toy Story* or a writer for *A Bug's Life*. Still, he did make a famous contribution to the architectural designs of Pixar's headquarters. His main goal was to get people out and mixing across teams and divisions. He wanted software engineers who specialized in light vector fields to be chatting with story writers and voice directors.

Jobs knew that great ideas would come from people with hunches bumping into each other, and he wanted to multiply the amount of hunch-sharing through the design of the headquarters. He said: "If a building doesn't encourage [collaboration], you'll lose a lot of innovation and the magic that's sparked by serendipity. So we designed the building to make people get out of their offices and mingle in the central atrium with people they might not otherwise see."

Jobs requested the building plans to contain one large atrium with offices all around the edges. Inside the atrium were theaters, cafes, cafeterias, and flexible conference spaces used for everything from hosting speakers to hosting parties. The design was already unique, but to this, Steve Jobs added his special touch: the atrium would contain the only set of bathrooms in the whole HQ.

There was immediate pushback, but Jobs fought back. He argued that the whole point of the atrium was to mix people to drive innovation. He was promoting one of the cultural precursors to building a culture of change leadership. The single bathroom prevailed.

Brad Bird, director of Pixar's *The Incredibles* and *Ratatouille*, told *Wired* in 2011, "The atrium initially might seem like a waste of space...But Steve realized that when people run into each other, when they make eye contact, things happen."

In Walter Isaacson's biography of Jobs, and for most commentators, this was the end of the story. Long bathroom lines explained in some small part the ongoing genius of Pixar's technology and films. But there is much more to how Pixar uses spaces in unexpected ways to promote creativity and continuous change.

The famous atrium was not just empty space. Pixar had a whole team for filling the space with creative social mixing. People met at the cafeterias, where they could eat free and discounted food. Pixarians could attend speaker series or films in the theaters. There are often events and conferences open to all. No organization can have the mantra "build a bathroom, and they will innovate." Someone also had to set up activities and events to pull people together, mix them up, and help them interact.

Both new and traditional companies often provide no physical spaces and designated time during the workday to enable professional, social mixing. Time set aside for socializing is considered a feel-good give away to raise morale and increase retention. However, from the position of supporting bottom-up change, socializing is a necessary investment in new ideas and innovation.

It is more common to rely on old-school "drinks after work" for social mixing to occur by default. There are many, many reasons why this is a poor strategy. Not everyone is invited or feels invited out. People often don't want to talk about work in a bar or social environment. A bar or social space is ambiguous: are people socializing because they are colleagues? Close friends? Potential lovers? This ambiguity hamstrings many potential leading men and women who might misread the situation, or who feel uncomfortable and avoid going altogether. Some people don't drink and feel uncomfortable in a bar or around those who are drinking. And while a little alcohol might increase one's creativity, too much and the next morning brilliant ideas, if remembered at all, are as fuzzy as our tongues.

We can't all rebuild our offices around a single atrium (and bathroom), so what can we do to design for serendipity as Jobs suggests? One of the best opportunities for professional social mixing during the workday is lunch.

There is such a thing as a free lunch

Getting a free lunch is often synonymous with the impossible, but in innovative tech companies, such as Google, it's a given.

Immediately a debate broke out among commentators about why these companies provided a free lunch. On the one hand, a chef-prepared free lunch looks like a fancy perk. On the other, some commentators proposed that free lunch was a calculated business strategy to increase productivity. They reasoned that if people leave the building to go to lunch, they spend less time at their desks working. Ergo, free lunch was a cunning trick to have people work more on whatever management had assigned them to do. And free lunch is a cheaper perk than higher salaries and Cadillac healthcare plans.

A smart idea, but it doesn't stand up well to scrutiny.

Raw productivity measured in minutes increases if workers are kept plugging away at their desks, but a free lunch takes them away to the cafeteria. If Google's management wanted employees to stay at their desks during lunch, they would do what every office already does. They would put a refrigerator, a microwave, and a coffee machine in each office suite. This way, people are prompted to bring their lunches and eat them at their desks. If Google's management wanted to provide a fancy perk while keeping people working, Google would have delivered food to people where they worked each day. But that is not what they did.

Almost every tech company in Silicon Valley, including Google, did the exact opposite. They said to their employees, "Stop what you are doing. Walk away from your desk and computer. Come to another part of the building. There you can eat free food and chat with your colleagues."

The famous central atrium of Pixar's headquarters, the one Steve Jobs insisted would have only one bathroom, also hosted the building's single cafeteria. History fixates on Pixar HQ's sole bathroom, but we have to ask now, did people connect more on the way to the bathroom, or at lunch? Something tells me the lunch line is a more comfortable place to get to know a new face than the bathroom line.

For a company to offer free lunch is costly in both time and money. Five-star chefs and grass-fed peppercorn-encrusted flank steaks do not come cheap. It takes time for employees to walk across campus to the cafeteria, pick their food, sit, eat, and socialize, and finally walk back to their offices. Providing a free lunch requires more time than it would take to eat a cold tuna salad sandwich or microwaved leftovers at one's desk.

If a free lunch is so damn expensive, why is it such a universal practice? How can companies afford to provide a free lunch and lose almost an hour per day of people working?

In the business classic *Never Eat Alone,* Keith Ferrazzi calls out the casual relationship building that happens around food to be the core of his career success. Free food is a way of inviting all employees to participate in the practice Ferrazzi recommends to advance themselves, but also to advance their company. As he points out, "a relationship-driven career is good for the companies you work for because everyone benefits from your own growth—it's the value you bring that makes people want to connect with you. You feel satisfaction when both your peers and your organization share in your advancement."

Ferrazzi spends most of his book explaining how building relationships will grow an individual's career, but he does not explain how these relationships advance a company. By building the Pixar atrium, Jobs is suggesting that these serendipitous relationships drive creativity and change. The casual, serendipitous mixing of a free lunch is the precursor to the change leadership that happens later in private conversations.

For any company interested in bottom-up change, free lunch is worth it. Free lunch pulls people into a central cafeteria, like Pixar's atrium. That cafeteria is the arena for the private and casual conversations that support the social networks that support innovation. If process improvement, product development, and new products are valuable to your business, free lunch will pay for itself.

Not every company is ready to fork out for a chef and a cafeteria for free lunch every day. But there are ways to make it more affordable. For example, People complain that Apple makes people pay for their food. Apple's lunch is steeply subsidized to pull people into their cafeteria. You can get organic sea bass fillet for a cool six bucks.

A meeting with free lunch might feel like it squeezes another hour of work into the day, but it doesn't provide the same benefits as an unstructured free lunch. Meetings with food don't have the casual brainstorming and social development that happens during a truly free lunch. Working lunch meetings do not enable social networks that underpin innovation in your company to grow.

A free social lunch is beneficial even if it happens only once a week. Make School is not as well-funded as other Silicon Valley tech companies, so we have weekly social lunches. These have led to more connections and some of the best innovations in the company.

Professional social mixing across job roles and divisions is an essential precursor to the organization cultivating a culture of change. Providing lunch is a proven way to enable it.

Nevertheless, the connections and ideas that spark out of this mixing won't come to fruition unless they can move into private conversations. Adequate privacy for employees is another pillar of building a culture of positive change and innovation, but most businesses are going in the opposite direction.

14

IN PRAISE OF PRIVACY

I n 2015, Facebook broke a world record. They opened the largest open office in existence. The airplane hangar space was their new headquarters designed by Frank Gehry and housed 2,800 Facebook employees.

Open office layouts have swept offices across the country. They have become emblematic of innovative techie companies. But of all the offices, nothing came close to Facebook's new HQ.

It was a cathedral to technology. The building was one large room that spans ten acres. A sawtooth roof and floor-to-ceiling windows flooded the space with natural light. On the roof was a 1.4-megawatt solar array and a seventeen-million-gallon water reclamation system. Exposed electrical cables snaked down dozens of feet from the ceiling to provide power from those solar panels to a sea of software engineers. Desks were mobile, and teams could move them around, whichever way they decided. Zuckerberg's desk sat right in the middle.

The building was a symbol of the ideals and values of the company: collaboration and connection. But would Facebook's extensive open office plan play a similar role to Pixar's open atrium?

Would that sea of desks and light promote mixing and collaboration, and provide a necessary precursor to leading change?

The drawback to open office layouts

Research by Ethan S. Bernstein at Harvard Business School found precisely the opposite. Bernstein found that open offices reduced face-to-face collaboration by almost three times. Open office layouts inhibit both social mixing and private conversations that are necessary for leading change.

Before Facebook starts looking for their receipt on the largest open office in the world, let's look carefully at Bernstein's research.

Bernstein broke with past research into workplace design that relied on subjective and unreliable data from surveys and activity logs. He worked with an anonymous Fortune 500 company (call it "OpenCo1") that had recently declared a self-proclaimed "War on Walls." They planned to transform an entire floor of their headquarters into an open office floor plan. Bernstein decked out fifty volunteers with a custom-built wearable device called a "sociometric badge" that tracks every sort of conceivable interaction.

This device was like a FitBit or Apple Watch, but instead of tracking your heart rate and steps, it measured when you interacted with other people. The device "recorded, in great detail, their [face to face] interactions: an infrared (IR) sensor captured whom they were facing (by making contact with the other person's IR sensor), microphones captured whether they were talking or listening (but not what was said), an accelerometer captured body movement and posture, and a Bluetooth sensor captured spatial location."

They got granular. The researchers defined a single face-to-face interaction if "three conditions were met: two or more badges (i) were facing each other (with uninterrupted infrared line-of-sight), (ii) detected alternating speaking, and (iii) were within 10 [meters] of each other. The interaction ended when any of the three criteria ceased to be true for more than 5 [seconds]."

At the same time, as their FitBit for socializing was detecting how many times people chatted, the researchers also collected the email and instant messenger data from OpenCo1's servers.

The researchers did not want their data thrown off by the interactions generated during the chaos of moving offices. The experiment collected data before the move, and three months after the move was complete to avoid "transition interactions," that would not be representative of regular day-to-day work. When they finally crunched the numbers, Bernstein and his team recorded over 100,000 interactions, 80,000 emails, and 25,000 instant messenger messages.

To their amazement, they found that face-to-face interaction fell by a jaw-dropping 72%. Workers had almost four times fewer face-to-face interactions in an open office layout. Before the redesign, people spent 5.8 hours of face-to-face time per day. After the redesign, that number fell to only 1.7 hours per day. On the flip side, email and instant messenger messages (IM) were going gangbusters. Email was up 56%, instant messaging was up 67%, and instant message length was up 75%. The conclusion of his research is crystal clear, and Bernstein put it quite frankly—"in boundaryless space, electronic interaction replaced [face-to-face] interaction." Bernstein replicated the study at another company (call it "OpenCo2") with the same dramatic findings.

Losing information richness

Bernstein's research looked devastating for open office layouts. But what if all his findings were a good thing? What if, before the open office layouts, people were having long talks at the water cooler, and now they were more productive? Bernstein checked for that too, and in a confidential meeting with OpenCo1 executives, he shared that corporate metrics for productivity were down after the redesign. The conclusion was ironclad: open office layouts put a significant damper on productivity, innovation, and engagement.

Bernstein chalked up the loss of productivity to a reduction of what is called **Information Richness** in digital compared with face-to-face communication. Researchers in the 1980s discovered information richness at the dawn of the technological age. Already at that time, people were beginning to experience a challenge with technology that no one expected. A team's efficiency and productivity dropped if even small amounts of uncertainty were present in their communications. Researchers back then concluded that "lack of clarity, not lack of data," contributes significantly to inefficiency within corporations. Remember, that was 1986, many years before the invention of email, smartphones, instant messenger, and all the other digital tools, which all represent more data and less clarity than phone or face-to-face communication.

This drop-in information richness explained the loss of productivity when OpenCo1 replaced so many face-to-face interactions with email and instant messenger. But why did an open office layout lead to fewer face-to-face interactions and lower productivity?

Supporters of open office layouts cited sociological research suggesting that people would interact more if they were physically closer and within view of each other. The researchers into OpenCo1 revisited this research to challenge it. "When spatial boundaries—such as walls—are removed, individuals feel more physically proximate, which, such theory suggests, should lead to more interaction." And while this theory "has been observed in contexts as diverse as the U.S. Congress, nineteenth-century boarding houses, college dormitories, laboratories, co-working spaces, and corporate buildings," the researchers found that the theory failed in the case of open offices. "Rather than prompting increasingly vibrant face-to-face collaboration, open architecture appeared to trigger a natural human response to socially withdraw from officemates and interact instead over email and IM."

People don't interact in open offices for the same reason people don't talk on airplanes, buses, or libraries. Other people can hear what you are talking about. Whether you are discussing the weather, your kid's piano recital, sports, or the next innovation, people don't feel comfortable being overheard.

Interestingly, while Pixar had its large public atrium (and its long bathroom lines), it did not have open office layouts. In fact, exactly the opposite. Pixar employees may have to visit the atrium to use the bathroom, but they each have their own private office.

The evolving case for the private office

On the first day on the job, Pixar employees receive private offices and are urged to decorate them in any style they want. This policy results in some fantastic offices, for example, that of veteran employee John Lasseter's, who has filled his office to the brim with Studio Ghibli toys from his friend, the famed Japanese anime director Miyazaki Hayao.

The optimal design for a company's building, office spaces, and programming involves creating an embedded tension between social mixing during the workday and private offices and spaces for private conversations. People's hunches bump into each other when divisions and teams break down in social mixing at lunch or in some professional, social programming. Leaders of change will go on to host private, casual conversations back in private offices or nooks. Creating spaces and employee programming that enables flexing between these two situations promotes the delicate dance that supports change.

So what is the optimal way to use buildings and office layouts to support this dance?

There are a few design choices companies can make to increase and balance mixing and privacy.

If you can, don't build open office layouts. And if you already have an open office layout, see what you can do to create more private spaces for people to work and meet. As much as possible, treat an open workspace as an area for library-style quiet work. Expecting open office layouts to be hotbeds of collaboration will only lead to disappointment.

Perhaps what's best is to follow Pixar's lead and give everyone their own private office. Private offices provide the best opportunity for people to have lots of face-to-face private conversations and do deep work. Without taking the research into account, private offices were isolating and expensive, but the evidence says the opposite. Private offices are well worth their upfront cost because they make people both more productive and more collaborative.

Decades ago, Microsoft was a leader in giving people their own offices. They cited evidence that private offices made people markedly more productive. A few years ago, they caved to the trends and started to build open layout offices. Recently they discovered that their open offices were not working well for productivity or collaboration. Now they are leading the way with new office designs.

In 2017 talking to Steve Lohr at *The New York Times*, Michael Ford, Microsoft's general manager of global real estate, said, "Microsoft has taken a test-and-learn approach. It learned, for example, that its early designs were too open plan, with sixteen to twenty-four engineers in team-based spaces. Engineers found those spaces noisy and distracting, and concentration suffered. Too much openness can cause workers to 'do a turtle,' researchers say, and retrench and communicate less—colleagues who retreat into their headphones all day, for example." Now Microsoft is experimenting with smaller, semi-private, multi-person "neighborhoods" of office workspaces, and creating many additional spaces like phone booths for calls or quiet, focused work. However, this shotgun approach of building many types of spaces is one way of conceding we don't know what to do. Does anyone know what sort of work environment would work best and be worth the cost?

What About cubicles?

There are always cubicles.

I took a casual, unscientific poll of about twenty-five millennial tech workers in San Francisco on the topic of cubicles. Roughly half were open to cubicles with a few hardcore proponents and a few hardcore dissenters. Cubicles have considerable social stigma in San Francisco. No one wants to work at a telemarketing office with wall-to-wall grey cloth cubicles full of people taking calls on headsets. The cubical supporters liked the privacy and deep work they would get in a cube. But even if people could focus more, cubicles don't provide enough privacy for private conversations. Bernstein's research would suggest that cubicles would not significantly increase collaboration.

There are also glass-walled private offices. Technically, glass walls provide soundproofing for private conversations but enable everyone to see each other, which ought to increase collaboration. It is hard to predict if glass-walled offices are an optimal solution, but the research suggests it could work. I have a hunch that glass offices might be the worst of both worlds. People in glass offices might feel too isolated to connect and also too exposed to build piecemeal consensus.

Google followed a more middle of the road approach. They used to have four engineers per office following Stanford's way of dividing up grad students. But when all four people are there, you might be creating the same turtling effect of an open office layout, but on a smaller scale. If one person wants to meet with a potential new node in a growing social network, they can't kick out the other three. One person per office is best since there are no barriers to peers dropping in. A case in point: at Epic, Nikolai and I both had our own offices from day one. We knew where to find each other, and we could speak privately about the next steps for Betelgeuse.

It is counterintuitive at first, but innovation thrives on privacy, and since open office layouts limit privacy, they hurt change and innovation. Nevertheless, everywhere you look, the trend in office design is more and more open. The War on Walls continues.

The next evolving trend is organizations that have the money, and are building many types of workspaces: small offices, large open spaces, and private nook-and-cranny spaces for reliable areas to work quietly or have a private conversation. With all these types of spaces available, people can work wherever they like.

Nevertheless, the evidence suggests that, in spite of the cost, nothing beats Pixar's private offices for all employees (even new hires). Maybe the personal office is staged for a comeback.

15

HOW INNOVATION OFFICERS FIT IN

W hen we looked at incubating change in Chapter Four, we saw a traditional innovation team that wanted to build an innovation incubator inspired by Y Combinator. They hoped this incubator would help people with new ideas cut through the jungle of bureaucracy and red tape in their organization. But what if a company decides to use a *nemawashi* approach to change leadership? How does the role of an innovation team change when anyone can lead change through piecemeal consensus?

When an organization is operating on the premise of bottom-up change, innovation team members become the coaches, cheerleaders, and the referees for innovation leaders. They provide training to beginners and encouragement to advanced leaders. They act like midwives for new ideas, helping others bring new changes to light inside an organization.

The policies around innovation can change to support piecemeal consensus. Instead of urging everyone to go to their managers with new ideas, they can go to the innovation officers. More often than not, people with new ideas will arrive at the innovation offices looking for permission from above, a budget, and a dedicated team to start their project. They might be either insecure or overconfident of themselves and their idea. Their ideas will need a lot of work to improve and build a coalition of supporters. The innovation officer's new job in this environment is to develop these intrepid or shy innovators so they can iterate while creating influential networks around their new ideas.

The officer can play several critical roles:

1. Coaching beginners

Innovation officers can explain when and how it's OK to start validating an idea right away, without asking for permission. They can coach people to start conducting some of their first casual interviews with their peers. They can role-play how to learn more and develop buy-in without pitching an idea too forcefully and scaring people off or inviting dissent. And they can explain how casual interviewing provides feedback and builds a coalition of support and buy-in.

2. Ongoing support

People sometimes call their new projects their "baby" because a new project is like a baby; it requires constant care and support. Innovation officers can lend a hand supporting fragile new ideas by meeting regularly with new change leaders to see how the interviewing is going, review their recommendation documents, and decide on the next step. If a project is not working, an innovation officer can help coach someone move on to their next idea and not get discouraged.

3. Help and support going over and up

For many innovators, going over and up can be the most agonizing and most challenging part of leading change, but an innovation officer can help here the most. Proposals often become popular at one level of the company, but stall out and do not reach higher levels. Innovation offers can use their experience and clout to introduce change leaders to people at higher levels in a company that can provide essential, testing, feedback, and buy-in. People at higher levels will feel more comfortable talking to someone they don't know if they have the recommendation of an innovation officer.

4. Choosing the right actions to take

There are so many ways to take action, and this is the point where people often need the most coaching. An innovation officer can urge change leaders to take deliberate action, but in the right ways.

Novice entrepreneurs and innovators often believe that their projects require enormous amounts of money and sophisticated tech. An officer can help them brainstorm creative, inexpensive, and low-risk ways to demonstrate the viability of their project.

At some point, an idea that is finding strong support will need some tangible assets or resources. An innovation team's discretionary budget can operate as an account through which the company can make some funds disposable for innovators when they are ready to take some action.

5. Defending and supporting leaders

At first, an innovation officer will keep the various ideas and recommendations that are percolating through the company private. As ideas strengthen and coalitions grow, officers can loosen the reigns on privacy and connect others to the idea. The alliance around a new project will begin to grow.

As an idea starts to take hold in a company, an innovation officer can provide context to executives and higher-ups who are only now hearing about an idea. Executives can develop their own opinions about the concept and provide feedback before they show their support. At this point, the innovation officer can tell the story of the validation and buy-in that the change leader has developed.

There might be cases where serious company resources are needed to validate an idea. An innovation officer can help unlock those resources without reverting to begging for permission from gatekeepers. By building a large coalition of supporters for the idea, it is possible to find a budget and resources to run even an expensive experiment.

6. Setting expectations and rewards

As an idea grows, the initial change leader might have to take a smaller and smaller role in the project. Change leaders can feel betrayed or feel as if someone is stealing their idea. An innovation officer can set expectations and help the change leader to see and understand the long-term trajectory of their contribution.

The innovation officer's last job is to track the impact of an idea and assure that the leaders of the change are credited and rewarded appropriately.

In every one of these aspects, innovation officers and their teams are critical to the innovation infrastructure of a company. Using the five steps, it becomes possible for innovation officers to use objective metrics to report on the number of projects in their pipelines, their statuses, their estimated impact, and their velocities.

Anyone and any organization can embrace bottom-up change without internal innovation officers, but having even one will greatly facilitate change across the organization.

16

BUILD PSYCHOLOGICAL SAFETY
FROM THE BOTTOM UP

In 2016 Google released the results of Project Aristotle. The project's codename came from Aristotle, the famous tutor to Alexander the Great. Project Aristotle's original goal was to find the key factors that make teams perform at their best. To explore this priceless question, Project Aristotle's team mixed and matched people into teams and then measured each team's performance and surveyed its participants. The Google researchers found that only one variable mattered more than all others. They called this factor **Psychological Safety**.

The researchers had various hypotheses at the outset of the project. One common belief was that the more diverse a team, the better it performed. The more perspectives there are in a room, the better the final product. Did the diversity of the skills on a team improve performance? What if there was an equal distribution of genders? Older employees and younger? More and less experienced?

When the data came back, the researchers were surprised to find that the diversity of the team did not explain the highest performing teams. The highest performing teams did have diverse members and viewpoints, but some diverse teams were not reaching their potential. There was another X-factor in the equation.

In successful teams, team members reported feeling safe when sharing their views, opinions, and ideas, even when they disagreed with the majority or leader's views. This was what the researchers meant by psychological safety. When there is a lack of psychological safety, people feel like no one is listening to them, or it isn't safe for them to share; they clam up and do what they are told. People who don't feel psychologically safe at first feel frustrated, and later apathetic.

Project Aristotle showed that psychological safety is the catalyst that enables the benefits of a diverse team. Different skillsets, perspectives, and backgrounds only make a difference if everyone on the team feels comfortable enough to share their thoughts, opinions, and ideas. If people feel uncomfortable or unsafe doing so, the team underperforms. Psychological safety was the dominant variable in the formula for creating high performing teams.

Ever since Google published its research on Project Aristotle, interest in psychological safety has been increasing, and recently, with people ever hungry for more strategies to improve team performance and innovation, it has hit a fever pitch.

Williem at Square

There are lots of reasons why people don't feel psychologically safe at work. The worst and most egregious examples are when prejudice, discrimination, and physical and sexual abuse is present. However, a more common reason for feeling psychologically *un*safe is not feeling heard, and more specifically, not feeling like you can make change.

So how can you improve psychological safety in a company? I was given an excellent answer to this question when I asked Williem Avè, the Director of Engineering at Square.

"If a boss or a meeting lead makes a big announcement, and no one is feeling comfortable disagreeing or providing feedback. Then they say 'I want your feedback' and all you get is crickets, that is bad. Crickets are a bug."

Williem saw teamwork as code that either runs well, poorly or breaks, and throws errors. For him, a meeting without psychological safety was like when code failed and didn't tell you where the code was breaking or why. In software, this is called a "silent error," and it is the most frustrating type of error there is. The first step to solving an error like that, William said, is to get more information.

Williem suggested that a company trying to improve psychological safety ought to start by asking folks to rate meetings when they end. Meetings with low scores became the error messages that managers and meeting leads could analyze before making iterative improvements.

Williem also advocated adding a simple question to monthly employee surveys: "I feel comfortable voicing my opinion at work and in meetings. o-very uncomfortable, 10-very comfortable." From these surveys, managers could see which roles, teams, and populations were reporting the lowest scores.

Once you had a few error messages, it was time to debug your organizational code. For example, Williem made a few proven suggestions to improve meetings:

1. Leaders shouldn't speak until the end

Leaders could take the air out of the room and close down possibilities if they went first. They could facilitate, but it was better if they only shared their thoughts after others had a chance to share.

2. Be clear about the purpose

Another good strategy came straight from Amazon's playbook. Williem suggests using the first five-to-ten minutes of a meeting for everyone to read a brief statement about the background and goal of the meeting. The document could be a list of metrics, a summary document, a product roadmap, or whatever. By reading quietly, people get on the same page, but they also get a little time to think and consider how they will approach the issue at hand and contribute.

3. Break the ice

Finally, a fun and straightforward improvement is to introduce social icebreakers to meetings. Especially in a large company, people are often in meetings with people they don't know personally, and having icebreakers makes them see those people as people. Icebreakers have the effect of lightening the mood, making it easier to work with their colleagues towards a higher goal, rather than casting them as allies or rivals.

While interviewing Williem, he turned the conversation around and asked me the same question I was asking him. What did I think could enhance psychological safety in an organization? My answer, you might have guessed, was to use build consensus before meetings happened with one-on-one conversations and written recommendations.

Piecemeal consensus and psychological safety

It is remarkable how closely related piecemeal consensus and psychological safety are, and how they reinforce and amplify each other.

People feel psychologically safe when they feel they can speak and be heard. The best possible environment for talking and feeling listened to is private one-on-one conversations. We feel heard when people come and ask for our opinion about an issue or question before a meeting, not during it. If they feel heard before a meeting, they approach meetings more openly.

Meetings where no one has built consensus beforehand are not safe. They are powder kegs. Everyone in the meeting wants to be heard, but there is limited time. People in these circumstances have two options. They can either cut each other off by fighting for speaking time, or they can stay quiet and not share. The participants get the impression that there is a lack of respect for certain opinions. The group team will suffer from a vicious cycle of frustration and apathy. Chatting with people for a few minutes before the meeting is an antidote to this negative feeling.

Participants feel safer if a leader has already built the beginnings of a consensus before a meeting begins. In this case, there is little chance of the meeting being tense or heated, and people speaking over each other. It is even better if a leader can bring a document to the meeting that outlines the feedback and solutions already gleaned from the group.

A meeting runs more smoothly when the participants have already reached a consensus through *nemawashi*. Everyone knows when it is their time to speak because the document acts as a script. Someone might start by presenting the main issue, situation, or opportunity. People can take turns speaking by referencing their contributions to the recommendation. And transitions between positions are natural:

- "Matthew shared with me an interesting idea...."
- "Alison had more to add to that idea...."
- "But, Cory, you didn't think that Matthew's idea would work, can you walk us through your concerns?"

Participants already know about the disagreements and can use the meeting to try to solve them. It is easier to respect opposing viewpoints when the differing views are already known. The session can stay non-confrontational and productive. Any issue uncovered before the meeting occurs will often either already be solved or be almost solved because people had the time to reflect on it in advance.

There is still room for discussion and shifting opinions. Participants might still uncover more information or change their minds or see an issue in a new light. Nevertheless, the risk of harmful psychological safety is lower. A leader that has already made people feel heard and valued has built the necessary trust to encourage full participation.

What emerges is a virtuous cycle. People share and feel heard, which leads to them feeling safer. When they feel safer, they'll have the courage to drive new ideas and changes. These new ideas and changes, in turn, make for new opportunities for sharing, being heard, and feeling psychologically safe.

17

A BOTTOM-UP COMPANY: AMAZON

Meet Vihaan. He is an energetic executive product manager at Amazon. He lives with his wife and young daughter in a modest home in a hip neighborhood in Seattle.

When I interviewed Vihaan, he showed me that much of Amazon's public reputation is backward. Amazon is not a monolithic company: instead, it's made up of independent business areas, such as retail, Amazon Web Services, Prime Video, etc. And, contrary to popular belief, Vihaan claimed, Amazon is run from an underwater Seattle lair by its fabulously wealthy, Lex Lutheresque founder and CEO, Jeff Bezos. At Amazon, Vihaan said, there is very little micromanagement from the top. Sometimes there isn't even very much macro-management. Changes, innovations, and new products in Amazon come from the bottom up, not from the top down.

"If you read the news," Vihaan told me candidly. "You'll see people say, 'Jeff Bezos is a genius and he is micromanaging his company and pushing his company into every vulnerable vertical.' In fact, it is the opposite. Bezos is enabling his team to come up with new ideas. Amazon is a company that supports you in coming up with ideas and finding the resources the idea needs."

"Jeff won't say, 'I want to enter this industry, someone go do something about it,'" Vihaan went on. "Every year you write a report saying what are you going to do next year. What would you do if you had the same resources as last year? What would you do if you had more resources? You can suggest incremental change, but it can also be big things."

Could everything Joe Blow on the street perceives about Amazon be wrong? And if Vihaan was right, what mechanism had Amazon put into place to allow new ideas to flow efficiently through its hierarchy?

The Everything Store

To learn more and confirm Vihaan's story, I turned to the book, *The Everything Store*, by journalist Brad Stone.

Stone, like many writers of business sagas, presents the story of Amazon through the lens of what historians call the Great Man Theory. For Stone, the success of Amazon relies almost entirely on the company's visionary founder and CEO. But in reading Stone's story, it's possible to see how Bezos started as a tyrant who micromanaged the fledgling online retailer. When the company hit a tipping point after the Dot-com Bubble bust, Bezos intentionally changed Amazon. He transformed its culture from traditional top-down innovation into one that innovated from the bottom-up.

In the late 1990s, before the dot-com bust, Amazon had around ten thousand employees and was struggling to organize itself effectively. Bezos, at this time, was at the tippy-top of a classic ironclad hierarchy. He and his executives gave orders and rallied the troops with slogans and numeric goals. People below took orders and stayed in their lanes. But Bezos was an unhappy king on his throne.

Stone recounts a meeting with consultants where they were discussing a restructure, where Bezos voiced his concerns about the company's structure. "A hierarchy isn't responsive enough to change," Bezos said. "I'm still trying to get people to do occasionally what I ask. And if I was successful, maybe we wouldn't have the right kind of company." Bezos was unhappy with the hierarchy's inflexibility, but he wasn't searching for a way to exert his will over the company. Bezos didn't want to micromanage his company better. He wanted to empower the smart people he'd hired to excel at their jobs and make Amazon great.

Stone likes to compare Jeff Bezos and Steve Jobs. Their fiery tempers. Their uncanny power of prophecy. Their childish tantrums. The colossal scale of their successes and their mistakes. But there is a significant difference between the two leaders. Jobs famously ordered his team to build an operating system, a music player, a phone, or a cloud storage solution. Bezos, on the other hand, wanted to ask his people—all the way down to the front-line managers—to find out where the company ought to go next. This honest recognition of the bounded rationality of a CEO and a small team of executives makes Bezos different from Jobs.

In that meeting, Bezos recognized that it was risky and inefficient for all of Amazon to depend on him and senior executives for ideas and direction. The dot-com bust almost killed Amazon; during that time, Bezos didn't have the time or impetus to make changes to the organization's hierarchy. But once the economy was back on track, Bezos made a series of critical changes that have persisted to the present day.

Bezos invents "narratives"

These changes together added up to a reliable mechanism inside Amazon's hierarchy to unearth and act on the newest and best ideas.

First, in 2002, Bezos ordered his executives to limit the size of teams to how many people could eat two pizzas. The adoption of "two-pizza teams" meant that meeting sizes shrunk, and large teams were broken up into smaller, more autonomous groups.

While consultants and savvy business theory trends were promoting cross-division communication, Bezos bucked the trend.

He insisted that if teams were operating effectively, they shouldn't need to have extra structures for cross-division communication.

Bezos hated office politics and would excoriate people (even his top executives) if he got a whiff of posturing or jockeying for position. He wanted to optimize teams and tone down office politics. In 2003 he had his "Aha!" moment and took drastic measures. Bezos banned PowerPoint presentations. He knew that presentations often stood more on a speaker's performance and personal charisma than on the merits of their ideas. In place of slide presentations, Bezos mandated everyone to writing what he called "narratives."

A narrative, much like the SBAR decision document, describes an issue or challenge and outlines a recommendation. Bezos believes that writing documents and reading them would make teams more thoughtful than turning up to listen to PowerPoint presentations.

Meetings at Amazon would no longer start with someone making updates and firing up their slide deck. Now, meetings would commence with the group reading one or more narrative quietly for five-to-fifteen minutes.

In 2004, after a few people submitted sixty-page narratives, a six-page limit was set with extra room for footnotes and appendices. Narratives use non-technical, everyday language, and authors write in the style of a mock press release to keep it focused on the customer experience.

After the last presentation holdouts gave up, narratives became a cornerstone of Amazon's culture and success. But narratives alone were not going to suss out all the great ideas.

I returned to talk to Vihaan to understand Amazon's mechanism for bottom-up innovation. Vihaan told me the story of Andy Jassy, a famous Amazoner who wrote the narrative that suggested Amazon own and operate its own servers. This narrative became Amazon Web Services (AWS), now hosting around one-third of all internet traffic.

The bottom-up story of Andrew Jassy

When Jeff Bezos founded Amazon in 1994, the plan was to become "the everything store." Essentially, Bezos wanted Amazon to be an online Walmart. The problem was that customers in 1994 were dubious of buying things online. Bezos and his team decided to start by selling books for two reasons: books are small and standardized, and the U.S. Postal Service would ship books cheaper through a program called Media Mail.

Books turned out to be a great place to start. Amazon rapidly ate up Borders Books and Barnes & Nobel as fast as Netflix would gobble up Blockbuster a decade later. But where should they go next?

Enter Andy Jassy. Jassy was an early recruit to Amazon straight out of Harvard Business School. He was not an engineer, which weakened his clout in the burgeoning technology company, but he distinguished himself through his ideas and leadership.

In 1997 Jassy had an idea and wrote one of Amazon's first narratives. He suggested Amazon should start selling CDs. Even though he wrote the plan, another executive was chosen to run with his idea. Vihaan claims they've changed this, and the new standard is "You write it, you run it." But while Jassy was robbed of being the head of Amazon's first retail segment outside of books, he would have more chances to succeed. In 2004 he became the first chief of staff to Bezos himself.

Amazon is built to grow people and keep them. It does not use consultants and promotes internally, making space for rising narrative writers. It does not succumb to the temptation of hiring ex-consultants or hedge fund managers to senior positions. External senior hires are usually either the founder of an acquired startup or a VP from another tech company. Anyone in Amazon is free to apply for any open job role in the company. Managers and divisions can't hang on to people who want to leave them. This intelligent policy keeps talented workers at the company and out of the clutches of Amazon's competitors. It also has the added benefit of revealing bad managers and poorly run divisions.

After being chief of staff for a year, Jassy had another idea and wrote another narrative. Amazon had been building up its own server infrastructure. Jassy was the first person to see the potential of Amazon selling their excess server capacity. Amazon Web Services (AWS) was born, and this time, Jassy got to run with it.

Jassy's narrative for Amazon Music and AWS became the mechanism by which Amazon sources and acts on the best ideas from around the organization. Vihaan told me this mechanism goes by the unassuming name of Operational Planning.

A meritocracy of ideas at Amazon

"Everyone wants to be a meritocracy of ideas!" Vihaan shouted playfully. "But at Amazon, they actually operationalize it. Crappy managers can't scuttle people's ideas. If they could, Amazon would not be the company that it is."

I pressed Vihaan for an explanation. How can Amazon run as a traditional hierarchy but still source the best ideas from front-line employees and managers?

At traditional companies, Vihaan explained, every year, CEOs and Senior Vice Presidents of most companies go into a conference room or to a swanky off-site to design a three-to-five-year strategic plan for the company. Maybe they give the new vision a slogan or codify it into objectives. They hand those down to their reports, who, in turn, hand them down to their reports, all the way down until they reach the front lines. People on the front lines make recommendations for how they plan to achieve these goals. They submit these plans to their managers for approval. Each level of management repeats this process, all the way up to the CEO and SVPs.

Vihaan was explaining the classic strategy for change like Tim from Turnstyle explained to us in Part I. The first phase of this traditional business planning we saw before is called **Strategic Plan-**

ning. The second phase is called **Operational Planning**. The only difference was, as Vihaan told me, Amazon flips this process upside-down.

In 2004, when Bezos was outlawing presentations in favor of reports, he also decided to flip the top-down strategic planning process on its head. Amazon starts with operational planning and does strategic planning second.

Here's how it works.

Halfway through the calendar year, in June, every manager in Amazon writes a six-page operational planning narrative. The narrative is about the following year and has two parts.

1. **Steady State** - What could you achieve with your team if you had the same resources as last year?
2. **Growth State** - What could you do come January if you had more people and money on your team?

Each front-line manager writes a narrative and submits them to their manager. Those middle managers set aside two days and read all their reports' narratives and write their own six-page narrative and send it to their manager. Managers turn in narratives rung-by-rung up the hierarchy until the SVPs and CEO receive them. Now strategic planning begins.

Bezos and his SVPs act more like investors on an episode of *Shark Tank* than the senior managers of a public company. The team weighs the ideas from the narratives that have bubbled up from below. If they have questions, they ask the original narrative writer to come and talk to them: no flashy PowerPoints, only face-to-face conversation and the written word.

Finally, Bezos and the SVPs pick from among the suggestions. They pass on some and green-light others. They update the budgets and teams, and new projects kick off six months later in January.

Everyone wants to be a meritocracy of ideas, and no one is

perfect. Still, for Vihaan, he had never worked anywhere that was more consistently a meritocracy of ideas than Amazon.

Neither Vihaan nor I have found another organization that has flipped strategic and operational planning the way Amazon has. The process was not *nemawashi* exactly. Still, around each narrative, there is a considerable amount of piecemeal consensus-making to help an idea get more support as it rises up the chain of the company. In any case, the story of Amazon's narratives is an important one as we look for examples of piecemeal consensus and bottom-up change.

CONCLUSION: THE FUTURE OF CHANGE

I have the privilege of teaching rising tech leaders in San Francisco. In one lesson on startups, I start class with a simple question: Why are there startups?

The answer often surprises them. Startups only come to be because existing companies are bad at innovation and change. If Hewlett Packard could have made a personal computer as usable as the Macintosh, Apple would have never existed. If Ford or GM or Chrysler were capable of making high-end electric cars, Tesla would not exist. If Facebook could have invented a photography-based social network, there would have been no Instagram. Startups only exist because of the failure of larger, wealthier organizations to innovate and make new things.

Most organizations barely change at all throughout their lives. If we are lucky, new companies displace older ones that have stopped working. Automated looms displace weavers, computer companies displace typewriter companies, and on and on. But often older companies stay the same and drag along like zombies. Like cells in an aging organism, they don't die, they senesce—becoming less potent and useful.

And many essential organizations are immune to disruption. There are no startups that can disrupt our city or state or federal governments. There are no startups that can disrupt the United Nations or NATO. No startups will disrupt the police, firefighters, hospitals, schools, and universities. All of these critical organizations are only going to improve if they accomplish it themselves.

And what if there were no more startups and all organizations had to improve on their own?

In October of 2017, Jon Evans at TechCrunch wrote an article called *After The End of The Age of Startups*. It contained a dire prediction: the age of startups has come to an end. What was next?

Evans points out the many signs that the startup apocalypse is upon us. There are fewer and fewer new startups each year. The low-hanging apps and websites have already been built. Future products, Evans predicts, will come from technologically intensive domains, such as artificial intelligence, virtual reality, hardware, and cryptography. The barrier to entry for new companies would no longer be garages and MacBook Pros. Instead, would-be entrepreneurs will need million-dollar labs and PhDs.

The next generation of innovation will resemble the one before the startup age. Forty years ago, only large companies like IBM and HP could afford the investments in research and development it took to innovate. Change in this climate will not come from the outside and disrupt large, established companies. It will be happening inside these large tech companies.

When anyone could leave their job and start a startup, it mattered less if change wasn't happening inside large organizations. But as more and more of the economy takes place inside large organizations, and as the barriers to starting new companies rise, being able to lead change from inside an organization will becomes ever more critical for each person's career and society as a whole.

What you can do

If the stories in this book didn't convince you, pick a small, risk-free idea, and try building a little consensus around it. When people I've worked with have adopted this strategy, they notice an immediate change. They feel a palpable difference. They go from feeling like they were slogging uphill trying to make a change to feeling like they are coasting downhill.

I hope this book has provided you with an easy to use, powerful, and unforgettable tool for making change.

We saw in Part I that the most popular and most talked about strategies for change and innovation have critical flaws. They have anti-patterns built into them that work against the goal of rapid and positive change. Strategic planning from the top down only harnesses the genius and ideas of the top of the company, missing out on what everyone has to offer. Hiring consultants is risky and poorly aligns incentives. Front-line managers know changes will take away their best people and threaten their budgets and turf. Expecting them to identify and advance change is foolhardy. Trying to make organizations as flat as possible and eliminate hierarchy leads to operational inefficiencies and a culture run by cut-throat office politics. Building an internal incubator is a beautiful idea in theory, but it is nearly impossible to deliver in practice. So what can you do?

Half a century ago, this was the question that innovators inside of Toyota Motors asked themselves, and they developed a process they call *nemawashi*, or piecemeal consensus. North American translators of the Toyota Production System into American management ignored or downplayed this critical principle. Piecemeal consensus is the missing link of lean, agile, and SCRUM—all forms of management based on the Toyota Production System.

Anyone in an organization can lead change by building a new social network throughout their organization. Changemakers no longer have to wait for permission from above or beg for permission from gatekeepers. To accomplish their goals, they can follow five simple steps.

The Five Steps of Bottom Up Change

Step 5	Take Deliberate Action
Step 4	Go Over and Up
Step 3	Write A Summary
Step 2	Start with Peers
Step 1	Brainstorm

Using these five steps, anyone can get an idea, begin reaching out to their peers for feedback and buy-in, build support that cross-crosses their organization before writing a proposal, and finally taking action.

Leading innovative companies, such as Apple, Amazon, Google, and Microsoft, are already, unconsciously, using piecemeal consensus. They've adopted patterns and policies that make their cultures embrace experimentation and change. I've explained some of those policies in Part III.

Any organization can rapidly operationalize piecemeal consensus by adopting these policies. Give everyone opportunities for casual social mixing during the workweek, such as providing lunch. Following Google's lead, try to balance the power and influence of management and executives with front-line employees and independent contributors. Take deliberate steps to develop psychological safety throughout the organization. Don't fall prey to the fad of open-office layouts that rob people of their privacy and eliminate valuable face-to-face collaboration. Try dropping presentations in favor of starting meetings with brief written documents and proposals. Consider what Amazon, one of the most successful and innovative companies in history, has been doing for over a decade, and aim to build your next strategic plan out of the bottom-up suggestions of front-line employees and managers.

Some of these policies might be radical from where your company is now, but others are more moderate and achievable. All of them will move the needle in an organization to support and cultivate bottom-up change and piecemeal consensus.

Every nook and cranny of our world needs improvement, and improvement means change. Permission paralysis doesn't care if an organization is for-profit or not. It strikes any organization that grows past even a handful of people. To succeed in making a good world, we need everyone in every organization to be successful leaders of change.

SELECTED BIBLIOGRAPHY

Leading Change, John Kotter, 2012

Never Eat Alone, Keith Ferrazzi, 2001

The Everything Store: Jeff Bezos and the Age of Amazon, Brad Stone, 2014

The Four Steps to the Epiphany, Steve Blank, 2013

The Hidden Power of Social Networks: Understanding How Work Really Gets Done in Organizations, Rob Cross, 1994

The Lean Startup, Eric Ries, 2011

The Machine That Changed the World: The Story of Lean Production —Toyota's Secret Weapon in the Global Car Wars That Is Now Revolutionizing World Industry, James Womack, 2007

The Startup Way, Eric Ries, 2017

The Toyota Way, Jeffrey K. Liker, 2004

Toyota Production System, Taiichi Ohno, 1978

"Reflecting On One Very, Very Strange Year at Uber." Susan Fowler Rigetti, 2017

"Uber's New Cultural Norms," Dara Khosrowshahi, 2017

Where Good Ideas Come From, Steven Johnson, 2011

Work Rules!, Laszlo Bock, 2015

ACKNOWLEDGMENTS

This book would not have been possible without much help and support.

Thanks to Kat Koh my wife for her constant support and feedback. Thanks to Nicolai Skievasky, now founder at Redox Health, who was my partner in change leadership at Epic. Thanks to Allison Carpio and Dan Morse who were critical to visioning, planning and positioning the book. Thanks to my colleagues at Make School and to Make School itself for supporting me and for working to change higher education. And Thanks to my editor Clare Grist Taylor, and to my friends on my launch team, for all their hard work and support.

ABOUT THE AUTHOR

Adam Braus is a university professor and educational program designer in San Francisco. He designs and teachers courses in Product Management, Software Engineering, and Philosophy. *Lead Change At Work* is his debut book about how anyone can lead change in any organization. He lives with his wife Kat Koh and his two cats Arlo and Elmer in the Mission district of San Francisco.

To contact him please email adam.braus@icloud.com.

Made in the USA
Las Vegas, NV
16 January 2021

16060547R00111